The Meaning
of
Christianity

by

Peter Nemeshegyi

Translated by Stephen Békési, S.J.
and Dr. Bernard Gilligan

PAULIST PRESS
New York / Ramsey

248
Nem

Library of Congress
Catalog Card Number: 82-81189

ISBN: 0-8091-2464-5

Published by Paulist Press
545 Island Road, Ramsey, N.J. 07446

Printed and bound in the
United States of America

Contents

I have tried in these few pages to answer for myself the question of what it means to be a Christian. I hope I have succeeded in such a way as to reach the hearts of my readers.

Tokyo
February, 1976

Preface to the English Edition

"And this is eternal life, that they know Thee the only true God, and Jesus Christ whom Thou hast sent" (John 17:3).

I believe these words of Jesus to be true. That is why I have written this book. Human beings cannot live without love. True and universal love, a love stronger than death, is manifested and given to us by Jesus Christ. I wish this love and the eternal life that springs from it for all my fellow human beings. That is why I am happy to know that now my little book will speak for me to my English-speaking brothers and sisters.

I first composed this book in Hungarian, and twenty-three thousand copies of it have been printed in that language and sold. I have been living in Japan for the past twenty-five years, so I decided to write my book in the Japanese language as well. Six editions and twenty thousand copies of the Japanese version have appeared in print. The book has been translated into Korean, and in this language, I am told, it has had a wide circulation. A German edition has recently made its appearance, and now, to my great joy, this English edition is being made available.

I am very grateful to those who have made the appearance of this English edition possible. Father Stephen Békési, S.J., parish priest of the Hungarian parish in Hamilton, Canada, wrote the first draft of the translation from the Hungarian language, and Professor Bernard B. Gilligan, of Fordham University, New York City, has given the translation its final shape. Both have done a splendid job. May God reward them for their generous labor.

St. Augustine has written the following beautiful words on the subject of Christian instruction:

Christ came chiefly for this reason: that man might learn how much God loves him, and might learn this to the end that he might begin to glow with love of Him by whom he was first loved, and so might love his neighbor at the bidding and after the example of Him who made Himself man's neighbor by loving him. With this love, then, set before you as an end, so give all your instructions that he to whom you speak by hearing may believe, and by believing may hope, and by hoping may love (*De Catechizandis Rudibus* I.4.8; translated by J. P. Christopher, in *Ancient Christian Writers*, No. 2, pp. 23–24).

This is exactly the purpose of this little book. I pray God that these words will become a reality for all those who read its pages.

Tokyo
Feast of St. Elizabeth of Hungary
November 17, 1981

Foreword

Christianity has been in the world now for about two thousand years. Christians can be found in almost any corner of the globe. It is not only in the cities and villages of Europe that church bells call the faithful to Sunday worship. Prayer—in Christ—rises up to the Father in the crowded churches of the Americas and Australia. Forty percent of the African people are already Christians, and their number is growing rapidly every year. There are small, devout Christian congregations scattered throughout Asia. Christians can be found on every continent. These Christians believe in a loving God. They thank Him for His goodness. They try to live and die the way Jesus did, the way He, their Master, taught them.

All of them know, in one way or another, what Christianity is and what it means to be a Christian. There still seems to be a need, however, for us to ask ourselves the question of what it is that constitutes the essence of Christianity. What does it mean for me to profess myself to be a Christian? It is true that Christianity is so simple that even a child can understand its essentials. At the same time, it is so profound that even the greatest saints and theologians are unable to exhaust its meaning or get to the bottom of its mystery.

Every individual and every age must discover Christianity for themselves anew. With the help of God's grace, let us set out together on this path of discovery. Let us try to discern the meaning of Christianity for ourselves in our own day.

The word "Christian" derives from the Latin "Christianus" and means an adherent or disciple of Christ. As the Acts of the Apostles (11:26) informs us, the followers or disciples of Christ were already being called by this name in apostolic times. The word is very fitting. It introduces us immediately into the essence of Christianity—Christ Himself. To know what it really means to be a Christian, we have to discover who Jesus Christ is. Why is Jesus called "the Christ"? What did He do, and what actually happened to Him?

Chapter 1

"Jesus, Called the Christ" (Mt 1:16)

The Faith and Expectation of the Jews

Jesus, the son of Mary, lived and carried on His mission almost two thousand years ago in Palestine, the land that is almost identical with today's Israel. Even then, the majority of the people of Palestine were Jewish, and the land which had belonged to the Jewish people was then under the rule of the Roman Empire, as was the entire Mediterranean basin.

The Greeks and Romans of the time realized that the religion of Israel was very different from their own polytheisms and from all the other religions of the ancient world. The God of Israel was a single living God, unique in the splendor of His majesty. Omnipotent, He created and governed the entire universe. His breath was the fountain of life. Statues or pictures could not represent Him. He transcended all human imagination and language. This mysterious God, in all His magnificence, however, was not far from His creatures. His eyes rested on all mankind. He extended His loving care toward all. He cared for men and commanded them to be good, to fulfill His will. He could become angry at the sight of human sin infecting a world which He created good. He became displeased when men forsook Him, when they tortured and killed one another. The unrepentant sinner could not escape His punishment, yet His mercy was limitless, again and again forgiving the repentant sinner.

The Jews proclaimed that this was the God who had revealed Himself to their ancestors. He had spoken to them, making a covenant with Abraham, their forefather. Through His chosen one, Moses, He later made a covenant with the whole Jewish nation. He promised that He would be their God and asked them to be His chosen people. He breathed His spirit upon His chosen prophets—Isaiah, Jeremaiah, Ezekiel and many others. God's powerful word spoke to the Jewish people through the prophets: "Be holy, for I am holy" (Lev 11:44). God was faithful to His covenant. There would even come a time when He would establish a new and more illustrious covenant with them. He would imprint His law on their hearts (Jer 31:33). His Holy Spirit would be infused into the depths of their spirit (Ez 36:27). He would send His Chosen One to be the covenant incarnate (Is 42:6). He would offer His life in sacrifice to save them from their sins. He would be the center, the very meeting-point between God and men. He would be not only the Savior of Israel, but a resplendent light, illuminating all nations (Is 42:6). There would come a day when God would create a new heaven and a new earth (Is 65:17). All the living, united with God, would find in Him everlasting life. For death was not God's doing, but man's. He takes no pleasure in the extinction of the living. To exist—for this did He create all (Wis 1:13–14).

This was the faith of the Jews. This invisible God, the God of the covenant, was for them the reality most real. He was a strange and very special kind of God, unable to be represented in imagination and at the same time so very human. Many people today believe that this God was merely a construct fashioned by an ignorant people in their own image and likeness. Is not the truth of the matter exactly the opposite? Is it not rather that it was God who, according to Genesis, created man in His own image and likeness? Is this not the reason why, in the depths of the human soul, there is the light of reason capable of discovering and understanding truth? Is this not the reason why there is the secret desire for goodness in the depths of every human

heart, which urges man on, despite his passions and his selfishness, silently telling him "Be good till death"? Is this not the
reason why man is able to love and even give his life for those he
loves? Is this not why every human being is an unfathomable secret, which nobody—not even he himself—can fully know? Man
is indeed the image of God, and God speaks to man in human
words. That is why man, in turn, can use human terms when he
speaks of God. At the same time, we all know, of course, that
anything we say about God, no matter how sublime, is still like
children's speech when it comes to making sense of the incom-
parable mystery of God's being. Isaiah already knew this when
he exclaimed, "Truly, Thou art a God who hidest Thyself, O
God of Israel, the Savior" (Is 45:15). The psalmist sings, "Thy
face, Lord, I seek. Hide not Thy face from me" (Ps 27:9). St. Augustine writes, "God hid Himself, that we might look for Him.
And He is infinite, that we might look for Him, even after we
have found Him!"

Life in Israel in the Time of Jesus

The people of Israel were well aware that its life unfolded in
the presence of God. Jesus was a typical son of His people. For
Him, more than for anyone else, God was the "All," the all-important "One." Nevertheless, at the end of the few years of His
public ministry, He found Himself in deadly conflict with every
group comprising the contemporary Jewish community. In order to understand Jesus we have to know why and how the conflict came about. The Gospels and other historical documents
give us a vivid picture of the Jewish community. The representative of the supreme authority of Rome in Jerusalem was Pontius
Pilate. In the north, where Jesus spent the greatest part of His
life, King Herod was in charge. Pilate, the Roman governor, was
a benevolent skeptic. But the only thing that mattered to him
was to hold the reins of political power and collect taxes. Herod
was the typical Oriental despot, licentious and cunning. He

ruled and lived off the Jewish people by the favor of the Roman power, stamping out any criticisms that might arise.

In Jerusalem there were also the high priests, descendants of the rich priestly families. They were the most important members of the Sanhedrin, the great assembly or council. They held their jurisdiction by permission of Rome. Their only concern was that the prayers and sacrifices in the temple at Jerusalem be conducted in a regular and orderly way, that the people punctiliously observe the external religious prescriptions of the law and pay their dues to the temple.

Then there were the Pharisees. These were a group of religious fanatics numbering in the thousands. All their efforts were devoted to the scrupulous fulfillment of even the minutest prescriptions of the Mosaic law. They were fully conscious of their own religious zeal and greatly despised all those who did not think and act as they did.

There were also the members of the various revolutionary parties, who were storing up weapons in preparation for a war of freedom against Rome. They vigorously hated not only the Roman oppressors but also those Jews who were ready to compromise with them.

As everywhere, there were the rich, whose only concern was for money. They enjoyed their money, luxuriating in the sense of security that riches can provide, with no concern for the misery of the poor. Like the tax collectors, who levied a handsome surcharge on the revenues they were entrusted by Rome to collect, the rich took advantage of the financial state of deprivation of the poor.

There was a great multitude of poor people—peasants, fishermen, small artisans—whose pressing concern was their daily bread, dreaming in their misery about a fairyland flowing with milk and honey.

Then there was a crowd of the truly wretched—the widows and orphans, the blind, the lame, the lepers and the sick. They remained largely uncared for, living a miserable existence on the fringe of society.

It was their faith in the God of Israel that in some way bound all these different groups into one people. In Jesus' time, however, God seemed far away from men, and their faith in Him was no longer a living reality in their daily life. The success of a Pilate or a Herod seemed almost to prove that it mattered little whether one had a lively faith. The priests seemed to be concerned only about ritual observance of the sacrifices. The Pharisees cared only for the observation of the minutest regulations relating to the sabbath, the time fixed for different prayers, abstinence from certain types of food, the number of tassels on one's robe, the washing of hands and the like. The Jewish faith seemed to be for the rich, who possessed everything. Or it commanded hatred as the revolutionary groups interpreted it. It seemed to forget about the poor, who were told time and again by the Pharisees that they were sinners and accursed because they did not fulfill the law of Moses. It was as if God were angry with the lepers and the sick, their calamities interpreted as a punishment from God. In the time of Jesus, as in our own day, God seemed almost to have disappeared from the scene. The thought could very well have presented itself in some people's minds that possibly there was no God at all.

The Teaching of Jesus

It was into such a society that suddenly a new voice was heard, proclaiming "The time is fulfilled. The kingdom of God is at hand" (Mk 1:15). The appearance of Jesus was nothing but a mighty outcry: "God has sent Me. Now, because I am among you, God is among you." For Jesus, God was all that mattered. Because of this, however, men were all important to Him—each and every one of them without exception. Each man was infinitely important to Jesus. It was not important that a man was of little consequence in society, poor, ignorant, weak, even sinful.

He was more important than the law, all the ceremonies, customs and prescriptions. "The sabbath was made for man, not man for the sabbath," He declared (Mk 2:27). The Pharisees were astonished, they were scandalized, by such a proclamation. Although it was forbidden, according to the Pharisees' interpretation of the law, Jesus healed the sick who were brought to Him on the sabbath. Why should it be forbidden "on the sabbath to do good . . . to save life?" (Mk 3:4). How could we let a man suffer even one day longer just because it is the sabbath? Jesus did not contemn the prescriptions of the law in the Old Testament. He did not, however, consider those prescriptions, according to the letter, the supreme rules of life, God's absolutely last word. The regulations concerning permissible and prohibited foods were not God's final word. "Whatever goes into a man from outside cannot defile him, since it enters not his heart but his stomach. . . .For from within, out of the heart of man, come evil thoughts, fornication, theft, murder, adultery, coveting, wickedness, deceit, licentiousness, envy, slander, pride, foolishness. All these evil things come from within, and they defile a man" (Mk 7:18–23). It all depends upon the "heart" of a man. His heart is "pure" when he loves God with all his strength and his fellow man as himself (Mk 12:30–32). And this "fellow man" is not only one's good friend, our next-door neighbor, our compatriot. It is every man without exception, as Jesus pictured him in His memorable parable of the Good Samaritan (Lk 10:30–37). One of the scribes asked Him, "Whom should I hold for a fellow man?" Who is my neighbor? He had placed himself in the middle of a circle. His only problem was about how much wider he would have to enlarge the circle for it to include his "fellow man." Jesus answered with a parable. A man, wounded and robbed, lay by the wayside. A priest from Jerusalem came by, and then a Levite, a servant of the temple, but they passed on without even stopping to look at the unfortunate man. After the priest and the Levite, a Samaritan, someone who would have been despised by the Jews, came by. When he saw the man by the side of the road, he stopped. He had compassion on the man, washed and bound up his wounds, set him on his donkey, carried him to an inn and paid for his keep. Jesus concluded his parable with a question: "Which of these three, do you think, proved neighbor to the man who fell among robbers?" The scribe rightly replied, "The one who showed mercy to him." Jesus then said to him, "Go and do likewise." We should not ask whom we should count as our neighbor. Everyone is, but especially the poor, the unfortunate, the wounded, the broken-hearted, all who are in need of our kind hearts and brotherly assistance. All these are included in God's command for us to see Him in our fellow men. We are asked to be true neighbors, to love others as we love ourselves. Their happiness should be as precious to us as our own. "Love your neighbor as yourself." Toward the end of His life, Jesus went one step further: "Love one another, even as I have loved you" (Jn 13:34). This is the new commandment of Jesus, His one and only commandment, which covers everything. Jesus loved us more than His own life. He lived and died only for others. To love as He loved is the precept of Jesus, the will of the Father. If we ignore this precept, all our fine religious observances are in vain. "If you are offering your gift at the altar, and there remember that your brother has something against you, leave your gift there before the altar and go; first be reconciled to your brother, and then come and offer your gift" (Mt 5:23–24). God wants no prayer or sacrifice without love. Even a priest daily busying himself in the temple of Jerusalem, if he lacks charity, is nothing but a repellent example of a man who is ignorant of the heart of God. This attitude of Jesus must have been a great scandal in the eyes of the priesthood in Jerusalem, so jealous of its own power.

But Jesus was not concerned about the fact that others might take scandal at His words. In the face of a society that considered hatred of malefactors in God's name a sign of virtue, He

threw the fiery sparks of His burning words, "You must love
your enemies." There can be no compromise: "Love your enemies, do good to those who hate you, bless those who curse you,
pray for those who abuse you. To him who strikes you on the
cheek, offer the other also; and from him who takes away your
cloak do not withhold your coat as well. Give to everyone who
begs from you; and of him who takes away your goods do not
ask them again. And as you wish that men would do to you, do
so to them. If you love those who love you, what credit is that to
you? For even sinners love those who love them. And if you do
good to those who do good to you, what credit is that to you?
For even sinners do the same. And if you lend to those from
whom you hope to receive, what credit is that to you? Even sinners lend to sinners, to receive as much again. But love your enemies, and do good, and lend, expecting nothing in return, and
your reward will be great, and you will be sons of the Most High;
for He is kind to the ungrateful and the selfish. Be merciful even
as your Father is merciful" (Lk 6:27–36).

How badly the members of the revolutionary party must
have taken these words. Even if they had the idea at the beginning that Jesus was the friend of the downtrodden and the oppressed and therefore might be the leader of their movement,
now they were bitterly disappointed. How could they ignite a
murderous rebellion under a leader who proclaimed that one
should love his enemies?

The Way of Life of Jesus

The charity of Jesus knew no boundaries. His deepest affec-
tion and concern, however, were shown for the poor, the oppressed, the despised, the derelict, the outcast, the sick. When a
leper, having heard of His power to work wonders, approaches
Him, He has compassion on him. He stretches out His hand,
touches him—something the law forbade—and, with a single
word, cures him (Mk 1:40–42). It probably was the first time that

a warm, friendly hand had touched the forehead of this poor
outcast, the first time in his life that he experienced someone
loving and caring for him. From the eyes of Jesus, for the first
time perhaps, did he discover that God loved even him. Jesus
manifested the same kind of love for all who were weak or fallen.
He was not disturbed when a woman of ill repute washed His
feet with tears of repentance and wiped them with her hair (Lk
7:38). He sat at the same table with the tax collector, who was
despised as a sinner (Mk 9:10). When the hypocritical Pharisees
disapproved, He sharply reprimanded them, saying, "The tax
collectors and the harlots go into the kingdom of God before
you" (Mt 21:31). Jesus could also be harsh—harsh with the
proud, the smug, with those who had no concern for others,
who hurt them, looked down upon them and despised them.

As for the rich, He did not hate them. He was not envious of
them. He pitied them. They were foolish. They piled up wealth,
telling themselves that with the money they had they could af-
ford to eat, drink and enjoy life. In an instant, however, death
can come in the night and they will have to settle their accounts
with God (Lk 12:16–21). All the wealth they had amassed turns
out to be in vain. The god of mammon, whom they had served,
will have played a trick on them. The man is miserable who has
no eyes to see the beggar lying at his gate. His purple robes and
fine linen will avail him nothing. His daily feasting will turn to
vanity. He will go straight to hell. His end will be in lamentation
(Lk 16:19–31). How unhappy the rich must have been with this
teaching of Jesus.

Jesus proclaimed the good news of God's kingdom to the
poor (Mk 11:5). He lived for "the little ones." His heart, His
strength, His time belonged to them. He had no home of His
own, no pillow under His head. He gave His all without recom-
pense. He knew well that men were not saints and that not even
the poor were perfect. However, He came not to judge, but to
proclaim repentance and to extend forgiveness (Mt 9:13). Jesus

was the kind of man who lived not for Himself, but for others. For Him, every man was a friend; every man was a unique, irreplaceable treasure.

The Heart of the Father

Why did Jesus live the way He did? It was because He knew the heart of the Father. Jesus knew and lived with the conviction that God the Father is infinite love. He is the Creator and Lord of heaven and earth (Mt 11:25). He is King and Judge (Mt 18:23). He knows and sees all (Mt 6:6). Above all, however, He is good (Mt 10:18). The God of Jesus is the good Lord. He is the one who clothes the flowers in the meadow (Mt 6:28–30) and provides food for the birds of the air (Mt 6:26). He is a God who cares for us, who numbers even the hairs of our head (Lk 12:6–7).

There are three famous parables of Jesus depicting the mercy and goodness of God. The Father is that good shepherd who searches for his lost sheep and, when he finds it, lays it on his shoulders. Rejoicing, he hurries home with it and calls together his friends and neighbors to share in his joy (Lk 15:1–7). In the Gospel of John Jesus calls Himself the good shepherd. He is the true image of the Father even in this respect. In another parable God the Father is compared to the good housewife who sweeps every corner of the house to find the one lost coin. When she has found it, she calls together her friends to tell them of her great joy (Lk 15:8–10). Above all, God is that good Father who waits day in and day out for the return of his prodigal son. Once the young man comes home, disillusioned and in rags, he embraces him and kisses him. He doesn't even listen to what he has to say, but immediately begins to prepare a great banquet. "Let us eat and make merry; for this my son was dead, and is alive again; he was lost, and is found" (Lk 15:11–32).

This is the kind of God Jesus knew. His heart became one with the heart of *this* God. The only reason for His Life, His only

aim, was to fulfill the will of this God (Jn 4:34). Now the will of
God is to love as He loves. He does not wish that a single one of
the "little ones" perish (Mt 18:14). In the eyes of Jesus, God's
love embraces everyone. That is the reason all men are infinitely
important for Him. Not one of them is insignificant for Him. He
does not inquire first whether they are worthy of His love and
confidence. He just loves them all unreservedly, in a self-effac-
ing way. He loves them the way God loves them.

The good news He brings to men is this: God is with you;
you, therefore, should be with Him. God accepts you as His children; consequently, try to be good children. God forgives you;
you also should forgive others. Receive God's kingdom as an in-
estimable treasure (Mt 13:44). Accept God's love with confidence, as simply as a child accepts the love of his parents. Have
confidence in Him. He listens to the persistent prayer of His
children (Mt 6:8; 7:7–11).

Jesus does not mean to say that the faithful have only to say
the word and God will remove every evil and all danger from
their lives. Just the opposite. The sons in God's kingdom have to
shoulder their crosses daily (Lk 9:23). People will persecute
them, throw them into prison, even kill them (Mt 5:10–12; Lk
21:12–17). Having foretold the sufferings of His disciples, Jesus
nevertheless adds, "But not a hair of your head will perish" (Lk
21:18). If they should kill you, this is really of no more account
than if you should lose a single hair from your head. Why? It is
because there is really only one thing important for men (Lk
10:42), and this nobody and nothing can take away from them.
Only a man himself could foolishly throw it away. There is really
only one misfortune for men, and that is not to believe and
share in God's love. This happens when a man makes of himself
the center of the universe, judging everything exclusively on the
basis of his own private interests and acting accordingly. If a
man lives for himself and not for love, he is already dead. Charity alone spells eternal life, the charity that is the fruit of faith,

the faith that God is love and that he who abides in love abides in God and God in him (1 Jn 4:16).

The Miracles of Jesus

The appearance of Jesus on the stage of His people's daily life came as a sudden shock. He taught them as one who had authority, and not as one of their scribes (Mt 7:29; Mk 1:22). His hearers noted this again and again. People were attracted to Him in a special way because of His miraculous healing power. The evangelists recount His miracles for us. Modern men are inclined to doubt and suspect these reports of miracles, but these stories are reports of eye-witnesses and are intertwined with the whole of Jesus' life. They cannot simply be left out of the account of His life. Those miracles were the cause of His initial success (Mk 1:45). His enemies accused Him of performing miracles by the power of the devil (Mk 3:27). Once they had made up their mind to remove Him from the scene, the main reason that they gave was that "this man performs many signs" (Jn 11:47–50).

The miracles of Jesus are indeed signs. Like the lightning which seems to break through the heavens, a miracle momentarily reveals to us that God is the Lord of life, that God, who gives life, is stronger than death and all its harbingers. It reveals to us that God is good, that He is near to us and hears our voice. The miracles of Jesus were signs that the kingdom of God was at hand. They constituted an appeal to men to throw themselves with unconditional faith into the hands of a God who was calling them. These miracles, like any other sign, find their meaning only in pointing to something beyond themselves. The sick whom Jesus healed eventually became sick again and died. The men He fed with the miraculous loaves of bread eventually became hungry again. The dead He raised to life lived their mortal life a few years longer and eventually they died again. If a miracle were not a sign, it would be nothing but a foolish attempt to tamper with an originally poorly constructed world. The miracles of Jesus were a sign, a call for men to believe in the divine word being proclaimed by Him: "I am the resurrection and the life; he who believes in Me, though he die, yet shall he live" (Jn 11:25). He shall live, not for a few more years, but forever with God. Were God to shower us constantly with His miracles, He would make it impossible for us to accept His promises with a confident faith and an unselfish, self-sacrificing love. To believe in such a God would simply be to pursue our selfish interest, and that would be eternal death. Only unselfish love leads to eternal life. That is why Jesus rebuked the crowds who flocked to Him after the miraculous multiplication of the loaves of bread in order to have Him perform more miracles. "Truly, truly, I say to you, you seek Me, not because you saw signs, but because you ate your fill of the loaves" (Jn 6:26). He wanted the crowds to believe, having seen the sign. He wanted them to believe that in Him God's kingdom had appeared in their midst. He wanted them to follow Him in the way of faith, hope and charity, arriving together with Him in the kingdom of the Father. But they were concerned only about their daily bread. Once they realized He was not willing to repeat His miracles for them on a daily basis, they became angry and forsook Him as a useless prophet (Jn 6:60–66). And so it came to pass that with the increasing enmity on the part of the leading circles and the disappointment of the crowds His followers were reduced to the little band of His devoted disciples.

Jesus and His Disciples

Jesus had chosen these disciples Himself. Most of them were simple fishermen from Galilee. They had left everything and followed Him. He chose twelve from among them to be always with Him (Mk 3:13–15). From time to time He sent them out to proclaim the coming of the kingdom of God. This is why they have been called "apostles," the Greek term for "those who were sent." When they returned from their mission, He kept them with Himself and together they wandered over the dusty roads of Israel.

Among the twelve apostles, the two brothers, John and James, and, in a special way, the person of Peter, stood out. It was Jesus Himself who had given Simon the fisherman this name of Peter, that is, "the rock." Jesus once asked His disciples, "Who do men say the Son of Man is?" (Mt 16:13). The disciples replied with the different opinions held about Him by different people. Jesus then asked them, "But who do you say that I am?" The disciples were afraid to answer. They sensed it was a decisive moment of truth for them. Such a moment comes in every man's life in one form or other. Will he or will he not accept this Jesus of Nazareth and thus determine his own fate? Peter stepped forward and replied, "You are the Christ, the Son of the living God" (Mt 16:16). In Greek, "the Christ" means "the Anointed One." It is a translation of the Hebrew "Messiah." This was the title given by the Jews in the time of Jesus to the liberator whom they expected, to the one who would fulfill the covenant and be the splendor of the world. Peter, therefore, was confessing that Jesus, this poor, unrecognized, abandoned teacher, was the long-awaited Savior of Israel. He even calls Him the very Son of God. It is possible that at this point Peter did not yet understand the full significance of his confession. But Jesus praised him, saying, "Blessed are you, Simon, because My Father has revealed this to you. . . . And I tell you, you are Peter, and on this Rock I will build My Church" (Mt 16:18).

Up to Jerusalem

This was something unheard of until then. The people of Israel acknowledged only one "church" or assembly, the "assembly of Yahweh," that is, the people of Israel itself. But Jesus was now foretelling the birth of a new assembly, "His assembly." At the moment there seemed to be no good prospect of its being realized. Just the opposite. The leaders of society had already decided they would make an end of the troublesome prophet from Nazareth. The Pharisees judged Him to be worthy of death, as a transgressor of the Mosaic law. The high priest of Jerusalem wanted to see Him completely destroyed as a danger to the religious establishment, that is, as a danger to the faithful observance of the religious ceremonies of the temple and the supreme authority of the priestly class. As for Herod, who already had killed John the Baptist because he had dared to criticize him, he thought Jesus to be a dangerous man, having no fear of human authority and basing His independence exclusively on His reliance on God. The position of Jesus was in opposition to the rich and mighty of His day, to the power of law and tradition. Against His powerful enemies He had no support other than His deep personal relationship with God, whom He called His Father, actually "Abba," which is closer to the English "Dad" or "Daddy." He spoke to Him in an intimate way when He prayed and referred to Him in the same way when speaking about Him. He knew that He was the "beloved Son" of His Father (Mt 3:17). "All things have been delivered to Me by My Father; and no one knows the Son except the Father, and no one knows the Father except the Son and anyone to whom the Son chooses to reveal Him" (Mt 11:27). These words of Jesus reveal the deepest secret of His soul. Such expressions as these, however, were intolerable to the Pharisees and His other enemies. They asked Him angrily, "Who do you claim to be?" (Jn 8:53).

The situation of Jesus became more and more dangerous. He could have hidden Himself and His little band of apostles, of course, in some out of the way corner of the desert of Arabia. He could have wandered off to regions outside Israel, as He had done for a short time (Mk 7:24). But this would have been to deny His vocation. Jesus was sent by His Father not for the benefit of a small group of the elect. He was sent to proclaim to the whole people of Israel, in fact, to all the world, that the kingdom of God had arrived. He therefore went up once more to Jerusalem at the time of Passover, the Jewish feast of liberation, when pilgrims would be gathered in the holy city in countless numbers. It was to be the last time He would make the journey.

Jesus knew what was awaiting Him once He entered this citadel of His enemies. He also knew for sure there could be no compromise. He knew He would not turn back. He would not use His power to work miracles to save Himself. He never had performed miracles for His own benefit. All His miracles were performed for the benefit of others. He knew that they would take His life, but He went up to Jerusalem all the same. Men did not believe His words. He would once more proclaim, and this time with the sacrifice of His life, what He had proclaimed during His whole lifetime: the kingdom of God's grace is at hand. God is love. He who abides in love abides in God and God in him.

As He entered Jerusalem, the enthusiasm of the crowd once more caught fire (Mt 21:8–11). He took no advantage of this, however, to triumph over His enemies. The knot of conspiracy began to tighten around Him. Judas, one of His own apostles, volunteered to deliver Him into the hands of the authorities. It is possible that Judas became a traitor because he was disappointed in his expectations. Like many others, he expected Jesus to become the leader of a rebellion against the Romans.

His Passion and Resurrection

A few days after His entrance into Jerusalem, Jesus once more and for the last time celebrated the usual evening meal with His disciples. At this Last Supper He expressed the totality of His being and vocation in a wonderfully simple and profound ceremony. He took bread in His hands, broke it and gave it to His disciples, saying, "Take this and eat it. This is My body, which is given up for you." After supper was over, He took a cup of wine in His hands. Again, He gave it to His disciples and said,

"Drink from this, all of you. This is My blood, the blood of the new and everlasting covenant, which shall be shed for you. Do this in memory of Me" (Mk 14:22–24; Lk 22:17; 1 Cor 11:24–25). The covenant that had been foretold by the prophets was then and there brought about. Jesus Himself is the incarnation and author of the new covenant. The sacrifice of His life brings about peace and unity between God and man.

When supper was ended, Jesus and His disciples went out into the Garden of Gethsemani. There, in the darkness of the night, Jesus was seized by the fear of death. Kneeling down, He begged His Father, "Abba, Father, all things are possible to Thee; remove this cup from Me; yet, not as I will, but as Thou willest" (Mk 14:36). Jesus experienced everything a human being has to endure, even the most dreadful agony of the fear of death. Even in His deepest moment of suffering, however, the word that was on His lips was "Father, Thy will be done." Hardly had He finished praying when Judas appeared with a band of soldiers and attendants. They bound Him and led Him away to the assembly of the priests. Here the trial of Jesus turned out to be a travesty of justice. The judges had agreed upon His death-sentence even before the trial had begun (Jn 11:50). In the midst of this mock trial, however, one magnificent moment stood out. Caiaphas, the high priest presiding at the hearing, asked Jesus the momentous question, "Art Thou the Christ, the Son the living God?" With perfect composure, still feeling the stings of the blows He had received on His face, Jesus stood before His judges, the seventy-one members of the Sanhedrin, and replied, "I am; and you will see the Son of Man sitting at the right hand of Power, and coming with the clouds of heaven" (Mk 14:61–62). Until that moment He had never made such an utterance in public. Now that His hour had come, however, He was unwilling to die because of false accusations. He openly proclaimed who He was and why He had come. Let that be the cause of His condemnation. The high priest immediately exclaimed, "He has blasphemed." This prisoner, who had almost been beaten to death, not only dared to affirm that He was the Savior of Israel, but also made Himself equal in dignity to the Most High God. That He should say He would be seated on a throne in heaven at the right hand of the Almighty was incredible effrontery. "He is liable to death," they exclaimed.

To condemn someone to death in Jerusalem, however, was a right reserved to the Roman authorities. The Sanhedrin therefore had Jesus brought before Pilate, the Roman governor, to have him pronounce the sentence of death. The reason they adduced before him was political rebellion, a charge without the slightest foundation in fact (Lk 23:2). Pilate, at first, did not want to sentence Jesus to death. He suspected He was innocent. Only after he realized he would be hurting his own political career if he did not accede to the wishes of the Jewish leaders did he finally give in. After a few delaying tactics, he finally pronounced the sentence of death by crucifixion. The soldiers led Him away, scourged Him and spat in His face, and then led Him to the hill of Golgotha (Calvary) outside the city walls of Jerusalem and there nailed Him to a cross.

For three hours Jesus suffered in agony on the cross. It seemed as if every form of human wickedness had descended upon Him to break Him. God kept His silence and did not intervene. He hid His face. What a terrible temptation that must have been. The devil, Scripture tells us, had tempted Him at the beginning of His public ministry. He tried to induce Him to use His miraculous powers to benefit Himself, to display His unique privileges before the crowd, to aspire to earthly power. Jesus emphatically rejected these temptations, even when they were repeated time and again by men. He lived as a poor man, simply and humbly, reflecting God's will and His pure love for human beings. But now he had to endure a two-pronged temptation of a very different sort. He had proclaimed, "Love your enemies," and now His enemies were taking His life in a most painful and shameful way. How could anyone love enemies like these? He always had insisted upon total confidence in God and He had abandoned Himself totally to God's will. It was this same God who now was allowing them to kill Him without moving a finger to save Him. How could one have trust in such a God? Such was the nature of the twofold temptation assailing Jesus in His final hours. The answer of Jesus was, "Father, forgive them, for they know not what they do" (Lk 23:24). These were His first words spoken on the cross, His answer to the first temptation. He loved even then. He had love for His judges, for His tormenters, for all, up to the very end. He loved and He forgave. "Greater love hath no man than this, that a man lay down his life for his friends," He had said earlier. And now He was giving His life for all men. For to Him, everyone was a friend, even those who betrayed Him, who hated Him and rejected Him. His last words on the cross were His answer to the second temptation. Turning to God, by whom He felt abandoned, He said, "Father, into Thy hands I commit My spirit" (Lk 23:46). With trust and confidence, with the obedience of a good Son, He then bowed His head and gave up His spirit.

His entire life had been one long hymn of love of God and men. His death marked the climax of His love. That is why His death revealed God's love so perfectly. What kind of person this "Son of the living God" was now became fully manifest. He was forgetful of self, abandoned to the Father, confident, taking everything as coming from the hand of the Father, giving everything back to the Father, of infinite goodness, wholly united with the loving heart of the Father. Even the Roman centurion at the foot of the cross felt this. When Jesus had died he cried out in astonishment, "Truly, this man was the Son of God" (Mk 15:39).

In the eyes of His disciples the shameful death of Jesus meant nothing less than the end of the whole story. He could not save Himself. Nor did God save Him from death. Was it all

an illusion? Such were the thoughts running through the minds
of His terrified disciples. In their fear they ran away and hid
themselves. It seemed to them that the mission of Jesus had
ended in total failure.

The Resurrection

But then something happened. It is something testified to
time and again in the New Testament. This event was the cause
that brought into being the world-movement which we call
Christianity. On the third day after His death, the terror-stricken
disciples were huddled together behind locked doors. Suddenly,
they realized that Jesus was standing in their midst. He said to
them, "Peace to you. Why are you troubled? . . . It is I Myself"
(Lk 24:36–39; Jn 20:19–23). The disciples at first did not know
what to do. They were afraid and astonished. Soon, however,
their hearts were filled with the certainty that Jesus had risen,
that He was alive again.

The first indication of the resurrection of Jesus was the
empty tomb found by some of the women who had followed
Him in His lifetime and who had come to the tomb on the third
day. What they had to say did not convince the apostles, but
only made them more confused (Lk 24:22–23). However, when
"He presented Himself alive after His passion by many proofs,
appearing to them during forty days, and speaking of the kingdom of God" (Acts 1:3), their hearts became totally filled with
an unshakable faith that "in fact Christ (had) been raised from
the dead, the first-fruit of those who (had) fallen asleep" (1 Cor
15:20). There developed from this an unwavering hope that "in
Christ shall all be made alive" (1 Cor 15:22). Not only the Lord,
but all those who believe and hope in Him, all who love Him,
can hopefully await our resurrection.

The first letter of Paul to the Corinthians was written barely
twenty-five years after the events of Easter. He presents here an
account of the eye-witnesses, Peter, James, the other apostles

and five hundred disciples, as well as that of his own experience on the road to Damascus (1 Cor 15). He had spoken personally and at length with the eye-witnesses (Gal 1:18). His account, even today, makes the reader feel the vibrations of joy that filled the hearts of the disciples when they realized that Jesus, for a short while the loser, had turned out to be the winner, after all. God had raised Him from the dead. Jesus truly is the long-expected Christ, the Savior, the Messiah. He is the Lord, mightier than all others, mightier than death itself. He lives with the Father and at the same time with us, invisibly, but truly, nevertheless, until the end of time (Mt 28:20).

The resurrection of Jesus is the fundamental tenet of the Christian faith. It has a totally different significance from that of Lazarus' having been raised from the dead by Jesus the fourth day after he had been placed in his grave (Jn 11:11–45). Lazarus could continue his mortal life for only a few more years. But the risen Christ will never die again. Death has no more dominion over Him (Rom 6:9). The resurrection of Jesus represents God's final victory over death. God is not the friend of death but of life. He did not create the world so that all that is beautiful and good in it should be turned into dust. There is nothing nobler and better than love. Love, therefore, and everything created by love, will live forever. In the death of Jesus love reached its summit. If there is a God, and if God is love, if it was He who sent Jesus and was worthy of His trust, then the death of Jesus cannot represent failure and spell the end. It could be nothing more than the beginning of eternal life. "Again I am leaving the world, and going to the Father" (Jn 16:28). With these words Jesus sums up His death and resurrection. He is going back to the Father, the source of all life.

According to Scripture, Jesus was raised in His body. At the same time, however, Scripture tells us that the qualities of His risen body are different from those of His mortal body (1 Cor 15:35–49). The laws of space and time no longer pertain to the

risen body of Jesus. Jesus enters through closed doors and van-
ishes in a moment. Our imagination, restricted by the categories
of space and time, cannot picture to itself what a risen body
would be like. Faith in the bodily resurrection of Jesus is extremely important, however, because it clearly expresses the
fundamental truth that the Christ who died on the cross and the
risen Christ are one and the same. Jesus of Nazareth, who
walked the earth as the incarnate realization of the purest love
for God and men, and who died, now lives forever as the risen
Lord. His love watches over us, a love that increased throughout
His life and reached its perfection at the moment of His death.
The body is the instrument of communication among men. The
resurrection of Jesus in His body means, therefore, that He is always in real, though invisible, communion with us. We are not
left alone. The risen Jesus is the companion on our pilgrimage.
In His resurrection, human history finds itself already fulfilled.
In the light of the risen Christ we are able to comprehend the
meaning of the whole of human history, the meaning of all creation. In the risen Jesus, through His Spirit, all men are to believe—freely and from the heart—in the love of God, and are to
live in His love, so that "God shall be all in all" and "God (shall)
be everything to everyone," and love may be everything to everyone (1 Cor 15:28).

The Coming of the Holy Spirit

The disciples began to experience the strength of the Holy
Spirit from the very first day of the resurrection of Jesus. The
Holy Spirit did not become incarnate. It is difficult, therefore, to
arrive at a correct conception of the Holy Spirit. Generally, the
presence of the Holy Spirit is felt through profound symbols.
He is referred to as God's spirit or breath. The prophets of the
Old Testament had foretold that this Spirit would be present in
abundance in the Savior (Is 11:2), and that all the members of
God's people would be filled with this same Spirit (Jl 3:1–5).

On Easter evening Jesus appeared to the apostles and, breathing upon them, He said, "Receive the Holy Spirit" (Jn 20:22). Fifty days later, on the feast of Pentecost, the disciples experienced the feeling of being filled with divine strength by the Holy Spirit. Moved by the Holy Spirit, for the first time they showed themselves to the crowd and joyfully proclaimed, "This Jesus God has raised up, and of that we all are witnesses" (Acts 2:32). Let everyone "therefore know assuredly that God has made Him both Lord and the Christ, this Jesus whom you crucified" (Acts 2:36).

With these words the disciples set out to convert the world. Eventually they suffered martyrdom for their preaching. Finally, however, their faith converted the people of the Roman Empire. The messengers of Christ today are still carrying the same "good news" to every nation on the earth: Christ has risen. His end was not a farewell, but an encounter. It did not spell decay, but a new blossoming forth. It was not eternal death, but victorious life.

Jesus, the Only-Begotten Son of God

It was only in the light of the resurrection that the apostles finally understood who Jesus really was. During His earthly life they suspected from His words and actions that He was someone surpassing all the prophets who had gone before Him and that He enjoyed the unique relationship of a Son to His Father. Otherwise, how could His appearance be considered a sign of the fulfillment of time, the beginning of the kingdom of God? Otherwise, how could He undertake to modify the law of God? How could He dare to forgive men's sins? But it was only after His resurrection that the secret of His being became clearly manifested to them. This Jesus, the risen Lord, sitting at the right hand of the Father, uniting the whole world to God as the sole Mediator, united with whom we are united to God Himself, this Jesus who sends us the Holy Spirit as His very breath cannot be a mere man, just a simple creature. Undoubtedly, He was a man. He was born of an earthly mother. He grew from child-hood into manhood. He was joyful at times and at other times sad. He labored and became tired. At one moment His eyes flashed with anger; the next time, they were fixed on a man with ineffable love. Now overcome with great joy, later His body is bathed in the cold sweat of fear. He died as a man. He rose as a man, to live as a man forever. But this Jesus is also more than a man. He is also divine. He is the bridge between God and man, both God and man at the same time. He is the unique Mediator (1 Tim 2:5). He is not identical with the Father, since the Father has called Him His "beloved Son" (Mk 1:11) and He called God His Father. But His very essence is, all the same, divine, and therefore He also is truly God.

He was divine not only at the end of His life, but from the very beginning. Paul, John and the others who proclaimed this faith in the early Church made use of the words of the Old Tes-tament. They spoke of Him as God's Word, Wisdom and Strength: The Divine Word exists from eternity with God the Father. The Word is the only begotten Son of God the Father, and the Divine Wisdom of the Father from all eternity (Jn 1:1–3; Phil 2:6; Col 2:15–20). The Word is true God because the Fa-ther "begets" Him, communicating to Him His whole divinity. The Word became incarnate for us and our salvation (Jn 1:14). God sent us His eternally begotten Son that He might live in the form of human nature. The very essence of His divine Sonship was to accept everything from the Father and to return all things to Him.

The Blessed Trinity

The profound and mysterious truth of the Blessed Trinity communicates to us a totally new dimension of knowledge about the nature of God: God is one, but He is not lonely. The very essence of God is an eternal streaming forth of love, a relation-

ship of love between the Father and the Son. The Father "begets" His Son, giving everything to Him. The Son loves the
Father, giving everything back to Him. The Holy Spirit is the
fruit of this mutual self-giving in love. The Holy Spirit is its very
form, the divine love-relationship. This is the truth expressed in
the mystery of the Blessed Trinity. God is one, but His essence
is the mutual love-relationship of three Persons. The first Person is the Father, the source of all good. The second Person is
the Son, the very image of the goodness of the Father. The third
Person is the Holy Spirit, the relationship in love between the
Father and the Son. Through the incarnation of the Son and the
mission of the Holy Spirit we are enabled to participate in the
very life of the Trinity. We have become the brothers of Christ.
Jesus Himself lives in us, and it is the Holy Spirit who enlivens
us with the breath of Jesus. God the Father accepts us as His
adopted sons. Prompted by the Holy Spirit, we can call God
"our dear Father."

The Redemption

This faith of the early Christians, given to them through the
inspiration of the Holy Spirit, shed a new light on the death of
Jesus. His death was not an accidental calamity. It also was not
the result of historical necessity. It was, instead, a perfect mani-
festation of God's eternal love for us. "For God so loved the
world that He gave His only Son, that whoever believes in Him
should not perish but have eternal life" (Jn 3:16). God "did not
spare His own Son but gave Him up for us all" (Rom 8:32),
"while we were yet sinners" (Rom 5:8).

All the powers of darkness had hurled themselves against
Jesus in order to extinguish in Him the flame of love. But every
sort of sin—the self-interest of the authorities in Jerusalem, their
selfishness, pride and arrogance, the cowardice of Pilate, concerned only for his own advantage, the betrayal of Judas, the
flight of the apostles, the coarseness of the mob, the cruelty of

the henchmen of the authorities—while tormenting His body and soul, He transformed into infinite love and forgiveness. As a man praying for His executioners, going to His death with love, for the sake of love, was the way God's Son manifested His existence in the created world. In this way He mirrored and brought into the world the infinite goodness of the Father. God detests sin because it is opposed to the very essence of His sanctity and because it is destructive of man. Nevertheless, here in this sinful world stands His beloved Son, killed by the hands of sinners, all the while that He loves and prays for them. Jesus is the perfect Mediator, standing as a representative of the whole human race. He is the perfect forger of a new covenant with the Father. In Him God finds, at last, a perfect answer to His call. God now looks at the whole human race through the Christ who lived, died and rose again for us. This explains why God sent His Son, why He wished Him to live solely in justice and love, a way of life that inevitably led to His death on the cross, and why He finally raised Him from the dead. He wanted to see us forever through Him, to see us as the brothers of His own Son. Through the crucified and risen Jesus He also bestows upon us the Holy Spirit, who might, as a fresh wind, blow away the dense fog of sin and illumine our soul with the sun of His love.

The suffering and death of Jesus thus becomes like the ransom money with which God liberates us from the slavery of sin and makes us His own (1 Pet 1:18; 2:9). He brands us as His own with the seal of the Holy Spirit (Eph 1:13).

The whole life of Jesus has become the way for us, the way to the Father, to life, to one another. Jesus goes before, and we follow Him. His death and resurrection are the moving force which sets us on the road and keeps us there until the very end. "The love of Christ controls us. . . . He died for all, that those who live might live no longer for themselves, but for Him who for their sake died and was raised" (2 Cor 5:14–15).

REFLECTION AND DISCUSSION

1. Compare the various groups and types of people living in our present society with the various groups and types of people during the time of Jesus. Are they the same types, or are they different? How would Jesus have addressed them? How would they have reacted to Him? To which type do I myself belong?

2. Jesus said that what is all-important is a man's heart. What is my "heart" like? What is my heart set on? Have I chosen unconditional, universal love as the basic attitude of my heart? Or is it something else that determines my heart's basic attitude?

3. Do I divide people into those who are my neighbors and those who are not, as the teacher of the Law did, or do I try to become a neighbor to everybody, like the Samaritan in the story told by Jesus?

4. Do I realize that when Jesus says "you" in the Gospel (in Lk 6:27–36, for instance) He is not just speaking to the people who listened to Him two thousand years ago, but He is speaking to me as well? Do I listen to Him? Do I respond to Him? Do I believe Him? Am I following Him?

5. Jesus had a preference for those whom He called the "little ones." Who are these "little ones" today? Do I, too, have a preference for them? Do I find myself by their side?

6. In His story of the rich man who put all his trust in money, Jesus refers to him as "You fool" (Lk 12:20). How does this estimation of money square with the way our society looks upon it? How about my own attitude toward money? Am I following the judgment of Jesus or the judgment of the world of today?

7. What is my own conception of God? Is it the same one that Jesus experienced and taught? Do I perhaps really have a different idea of God? Do I really believe God cares for me, knows my name, loves me? Do I believe God feels the same way about every single human being? Does this belief actually have an impact on my life and conduct?

8. Am I earnestly seeking to discover the will of God in my life? Do I consider the discovery and fulfillment of God's will to be the most important thing in my life? How can I, today, discover the will of God?

9. Do I place conditions on my following of Christ—miracles, for example, or success in my undertakings, good health, freedom from suffering, and the like—or am I willing to follow Christ unconditionally?

10. Christians believe that Christ's death and resurrection are the center of history. Are they also the center of my own life? If Christ had not died and risen, would my daily life change in any way? Do I face up to the problems of sin and death, or do I try to dodge them? How do Christ's death and resurrection provide a solution to these problems?

11. What is my attitude toward suffering? Should we accept or try to eliminate suffering? God does not love death, but life. Why, then, was it God's will that Jesus should die? Why does His death redound to life? Am I in the habit of relating my own and other people's suffering to the cross of Christ? Do I see His passion continuing in us?

12. Are we—am I—"Easter people"? Is our song the "Alleluia"? How is it possible to follow St. Paul's exhortation: "Rejoice *always* in the Lord" (Phil 4:4)?

13. Make a list of the texts in the New Testament which speak about the Holy Spirit (the Spirit of God, the Spirit of Christ, the Spirit of the Son, the Spirit of Truth, etc.). Try to discern what actions and attitudes are connected with His presence and work. Reflect and try to discover whether or not these actions and attitudes—"the fruit of the Spirit" (Gal 5:22)—are manifested in your own life.

14. What relation has the mystery of the Holy Trinity to the facts of creation and redemption, to our relation with God, to the "new commandment" of love and eternal life?

15. Jesus declared that He was the "way." Am I walking on this "way"? Or am I walking on some other way? Is this way leading somewhere? What is my answer to the various invitations for me to walk on ways that are not identified with Jesus? Am I able, with St. Peter, to say to Jesus, "Lord, to whom should we go? You have the words of eternal life"?

Chapter 2

The People of God

Jesus Lives in Us

Jesus died, was raised and has sent His Holy Spirit "to gather into one the children of God who are scattered about" (Jn 11:52). The risen Lord gave a commission to His apostles: "Go . . . make disciples of all nations . . . and lo, I am with you always, to the close of the age" (Mt 28:19–20). He had prayed for this at the Last Supper: "I do not pray for these only [the disciples], but also for those who believe in Me through their word, that they may all be one; even as Thou, Father, art one in Me, and I in Thee, that they also may be in us, so that the world may believe that Thou has sent Me . . . I in them and Thou in Me, that they may become perfectly one" (Jn 17:20–23). "I in them"—the risen Jesus lives in us and fills us with His Holy Spirit. This is the immeasurable grace given by God to the faithful of the new covenant: He gives us Himself. We thus become members of God's household, children of the Father, the brothers of Jesus and members of His body, the living temple of the Holy Spirit. This new life given us by Christ and the Holy Spirit is manifested in faith, love and hope.

Faith

The Christian life is one of a personal relationship with God. To believe in God, to abandon oneself to Him with complete trust in His goodness, to rely upon His word, these are the fundamental attitudes of the Christian believer. The First Epistle of John says, "We know and believe the love God has for us" (1 Jn 4:16). It is God Himself who speaks to us in the words, life, death and resurrection of Jesus Christ. God is telling us, "Believe that I am with you, that you are important to Me. Believe that your life will never be lost if you commit it to Me. Believe that I am Eternal Love." He asks us, "Do you believe this?" When a man answers this call with his "yes," he has faith. He then proceeds to build his entire life on the word and faithfulness of God. He puts his life and death in God's hands. Faith is not a theoretical acceptance of certain ideas. It is a decision that transforms our life. A man is capable of this decision only when the Holy Spirit enkindles a spark of His light in the depths of his heart. It is the Holy Spirit who makes it possible for him to recognize in the blood-stained face of the crucified Jesus the splendor of God's victorious love (2 Cor 4:6). The man whose soul has thus been attuned to God by the Holy Spirit joins in the chorus of Christians of all ages. It is not a human effort which causes the words of the Gospel to touch the depths of our heart. It is rather the work of God, "who opens our hearts" (Acts 16:14).

God's grace makes its entry with difficulty if a man's heart is proud, if he is conceited, interested in self-glorification, focused only on self-interest or assured that he "knows it all." The Holy Spirit enters and fills the souls of those who sincerely desire the truth, who "hunger and thirst for righteousness" (Mt 5:6). Jesus tells us, "No one can come to Me unless the Father who sent Me draws him" and "Everyone who has heard and learned from the Father comes to Me" (Jn 6:44–45). Faith is a gracious gift of God. It is at the same time, however, a deeply personal decision of man. Man is not "forced" to believe in God, neither by miracles nor by the promptings of the Holy Spirit. Signs only assure the unprejudiced man that the decision to accept Jesus is a reasonable one. But only he will believe who has made up his mind to throw himself into the outstretched hands of God. Faith, therefore, is constantly exposed to temptation. There are so many things that happen in this world that seem to contradict the goodness of God. But once a person has been made "His own" (Phil 3:12) by Jesus Christ and clings to Jesus there is no force that can tear him apart from Him. To believe in the heart of Jesus, in the love of God the Father, in the final victory of love, no matter what happens, such is and has always been the unshakable profession of faith of the true Christian.

The individual Christian believes, but he is not alone in his belief. From the time of Peter and Paul, through the ages, innumerable fellow Christians, brothers and sisters in the faith, till the end of time, walk the same road of pilgrimage. It is not just "I believe," but "We believe." This "we" vibrates in the souls of millions of our brothers and sisters in the faith over all the continents of the earth. We believe in the same God, the same Christ, the same Holy Spirit. We stand firmly together on the rock foundation of God's faithfulness. Together we have found the key to the meaning of the whole universe. The word of God, which we have accepted in faith, is not a series of abstract statements linked together without any internal coherence and far removed from concrete life. It is an organic whole, and its focal point sheds light on the totality of reality. This focal point can be formulated in different ways, but it always comes to the same thing. Jesus Himself expressed it in His words, "The kingdom of God is at hand." St. Paul expresses it when he says, "Jesus our Lord . . . was put to death for our trespasses and raised for our justification" (Rom 4:25). St. John tells us, "God is love, and he who abides in love abides in God" (1 Jn 4:16) and further declares, "He does not come into judgment, but has passed from death into life" (Jn 5:24). The Second Vatican Council employed the following formula: "God is with us. He liberates us from the darkness of sin and death and raises us to eternal life." In modern times, the "Creed" of apostolic times confesses, "I believe in God, the Father almighty, Creator of the universe. I believe in

Jesus Christ, His Son, our Lord, who became man for us, died and was raised from the dead. I believe in the Holy Spirit. I believe in the Church, the forgiveness of sins, the resurrection, and eternal life." It could also be expressed in this way: God the Father, by sending His Son Jesus Christ and the Holy Spirit, has given Himself to us in order that we might believe in His love, love Him the way He loves us and, led by the Holy Spirit, may, in Jesus Christ, come to share eternally in the divine life.

Love

When a man believes with total conviction, divine love springs up in his heart as a natural consequence of his faith. St. Paul, writing to the Galatians, says that only faith is of avail, "faith working through love" (Gal 5:6). Genuine love springs from faith: that is all. It is almost impossible to express it in words. Only those who experience it know it. If someone should ask what it means to love with this genuine love, the best one can do is to point to Jesus, to His life and death. The answer is in what is to be seen there. True love is to be united with the heart of God, the God who loves in an infinite way. "If God so loved us, we also ought to love one another" (1 Jn 4:11). We must love from our heart, not with empty words, but with deeds. We must be ready to lay down our lives for our fellow men. True love excludes no one, not even one's enemies. The one who truly loves suffers because of the malice of evil people, but he never on that account hates them. He does good to them and desires their true happiness. Such unconditioned love man cannot possess through his own efforts. Man will love truly when, guided by the Holy Spirit, he believes that Jesus "loved me and gave Himself for me" (Gal 2:20) and that He loves all men with the same kind of love. Everyone for whom Christ died, therefore, is my brother (1 Cor 8:11). We will love truly only when "God's love has been poured into our hearts through the Holy Spirit who has been given to us" (Rom 5:5). A man in whom

Christ and the Holy Spirit do not dwell will envy others, hate them, resent them, take pleasure in the misfortunes that befall them and be jealous of them. He will use others merely as a means for his own interest and pleasure. His personal ambition absorbs all his attention. He cannot see the tears in the eyes of his fellow man. He is unconcerned about other people's troubles. It is already something if he is content to take only "a tooth for a tooth, and an eye for an eye" and does not murder the person who may have broken his tooth or gouged out his eye. To love others the way Jesus did becomes possible for us only when the Holy Spirit permeates ever more deeply our whole being.

No one has described this love better than St. Paul in his hymn of love in the First Letter to the Corinthians: "Love is patient and kind. Love is not jealous or boastful; it is not arrogant or rude. Love does not insist on its own way; it is not irritable or resentful. Love bears all things, believes all things, hopes all things, endures all things" (1 Cor 13:4–7).

In his Letter to the Galatians, he writes: "The fruit of the Spirit is love, joy, peace, patience, kindness, goodness, faithfulness, gentleness, self-control" (Gal 5:22). True love contains within itself the fulfillment in joy of all the commandments of God. St. Paul rightly declares: "The commandments, 'You shall not commit adultery, you shall not murder, you shall not steal, you shall not covet,' and any other commandment there may be are all summed up in this: 'You shall love your neighbor as yourself' " (Rom 13:9). The ten commandments can be summed up as being nothing else but love, a life of love.

There is no stronger bond than that of love. Yet love is not bondage. There can be no stricter service than that commanded by love. Yet love is perfect freedom. There is no greater suffering than that caused by love. Yet love is the greatest joy. There is nothing that makes a man more vulnerable than love. Yet love is the mightiest power. In the final analysis, it is only love that counts, because love is life eternal.

Hope

Christian hope is nothing but this firm conviction that love is eternal. Its foundation is our faith in God's love and Christ's resurrection. Because God is love and the Lord is risen, we know that nothing is in vain, that eternal life has already begun, that love is stronger than death. We know that our faithful God will create a new heaven and a new earth. The fruit of every seed planted by the Holy Spirit will be ripened by the sun. We know that by living and working for justice, freedom and love on this earth, in a mysterious way we are preparing a fraternal community which will finally be realized in the eternal kingdom of God. We know that God is with us. Through us, He is leading His created world toward a state of final perfection. We believe that, in life or death, we belong to God. We believe that we who love another in God, even if we die, shall live. This is our hope, and this "hope does not disappoint us" (Rom 5:5) because it is based on the faithfulness of God, the resurrection of Christ and the divine strength of the Holy Spirit. Hope is like the tiny light of a small lamp that is nourished with the oil of the Holy Spirit. The darkness of the world all around it cannot extinguish it. Even if the darkness takes on gigantic proportions, once it reaches the vicinity of this tiny light, it turns out to be nothing. The light is much stronger than the darkness. This hope is a wonderful light. No disappointments, no failures, no matter how many, can succeed in extinguishing it. It has been sustained and nourished by an immense power through the ages—the power of God's Holy Spirit.

The Church

Faith, hope and charity: to believe together, inflamed by mutual love, to love everyone, to hope that we shall reach the home of the Father—this is the life-pattern of God's household. From its very beginning, Christianity established small communities of faith, hope and charity, as a result of the preaching of the apostles. Each of these congregations called itself "an assembly of Christ," using the Greek term for assembly, "ecclesia." The assembly of Christ, the Ecclesia, the Church, is nothing more than the little communities of those who believe in Christ, called together and enlivened by the Holy Spirit. The head of the Church is Christ, and the faithful are the members of His body, united with Christ, their Head (1 Cor 12:13). The same Spirit moves everyone in His own way. It is the Spirit who is the fundamental bond of the community. The Church is God's new people. The chosen people is no longer a special race, as in Old Testament times. Now it is the assembly, from all the nations of the world, of those who are united in faith. This is the fruit of Christ's redeeming death and of the grace of the Holy Spirit. Each member is a son of God, free and equal in his Christian dignity before God. The constitution of this new people is the commandment of Christ: "Love one another as I have loved you." The Church is spread over the entire globe. It is actualized wherever Christians assemble to hear the word of God, to commemorate Christ's Last Supper, to confess their faith together, to nourish their love and to enkindle their hope. However small or poor the congregation, Christ is there, and His Church is present in it. Christ Himself said, "Where two or three are gathered in My name, there am I in the midst of them" (Mt 18:20).

Tradition and Scripture

The preaching of the Gospel of Jesus Christ is what brings people together into the Church. That is why, from the very beginning, the Church took such special care to preserve and hand on intact the teaching of Christ entrusted to it (1 Tim 6:20). In this way the "apostolic tradition" was kept alive from generation to generation. This tradition has its source in Jesus Himself. It is founded on the teaching and preaching of the apostles. Like a mighty stream, it flows through the centuries under the aegis of the Holy Spirit, who keeps the Church alive. It is manifested in the whole life of the Church, in its prayer and teaching.

It was God's will, however, that the essence of Christ's Gospel not only be kept alive through the spoken word, but that it should also be committed to writing in Scripture. Under the inspiration of the Holy Spirit, certain men chosen by God were moved to commit it to writing. Their writings constitute what is called the New Testament. The Jewish people already had a collection of writings, which they called "the holy book." They considered these writings to be inspired by God's Spirit, and they accepted them as the supreme authority for the regulation of their life. Jesus Himself considered these writings as inspired by the Holy Spirit (Mt 22:43; Lk 22:37). But for Jesus they were not yet the final word of God to the human race. Many things found in these writings were not perfect. They had only temporary significance. There were even parts of the Bible which, in the words of Jesus Himself, reflected the hardness of men's hearts (Mt 19:8). That is why He opposed His own teaching to the regulations "given to the ancients" (Mt 5:21–42). In the light of the new covenant fulfilled in Jesus, the covenant of Moses became the "old covenant" and the writings containing it the "Old Testament." God's final word is actually the Word Incarnate: Jesus Christ (Heb 1:2). In the same way, the books of the New Testament, which tell of His life and teachings, represent the climax and the key to the interpretation of the whole Bible. The Church as a whole, under the guidance of the Holy Spirit, came to recognize the following books as constituting the New Testament: the four Gospels, the Acts of the Apostles, the twenty-four apostolic letters, most of them written by St. Paul, and the Book of Revelation. Just as a man with a good ear for music immediately recognizes the work of a great composer, so the Church, its hearing sharpened by the action of the Holy Spirit, recognized in these writings the voice of its Divine Spouse.

The whole Bible, both the Old Testament and the New Testament, has been an immeasurable treasure trove of the Church. In the past two thousand years, the Bible has been copied and printed numberless times. It has been translated into every language spoken in the world. Even today it is still the most frequently read book in the world. Even in a country like Japan, where the majority is not Christian, the Bible is sold at the yearly rate of three million copies.

It was written thousands of years ago, and it is still new and fresh. For innumerable people today it is the light of their earthly pilgrimage and a source of their consolation and joy. The Bible, of course, is not to be viewed as a book of natural science. It is also not an historical work. It is a religious book. With respect to matters of natural science, the authors of the Bible are men who think and write according to the opinions of their age. But when it is a matter of encountering God and attaining our salvation, they are the surest of guides. In and through Scripture, God speaks to His children and Christ teaches His brothers. In Scripture, everyone can find the way of faith, hope and love, the way which leads to eternal life.

The Apostles and Their Successors

Christ gave His Church another assurance of continuing the Master's Gospel and of perpetuating a living contact with Him until the end of time. This assurance is to be found in the original group of the apostles and their successors. Jesus did not write a book to preserve His teaching for ages to come. Instead, He gathered around Himself a group of disciples to be witnesses of His life, death and resurrection. He sent His disciples as His emissaries into the whole world: "As the Father has sent Me, even so I send you" (Jn 20:21); "He who hears you hears Me" (Lk 10:16). He commanded them to teach all nations (Mt 20:20).

This apostolic mission, originating with Christ Himself, belongs to the very nature of the Church. It was to be continued until the end of time. The apostles, therefore, were concerned to find co-workers and successors. In the beginning, there was no single expression agreed upon to designate an apostolic successor. From the second century on, however, the successors to the apostolic office became known everywhere as bishops (*episcopi*) and their co-workers as priests (presbyters, elders). Their commission was to preach the good news of Jesus Christ to all, to lead and hold together, as good shepherds, the flock of the faithful, to offer sacrifice—the sacrifice of the Mass—in the name of Christ, and to administer the sacraments.

The New Testament tells us that the co-workers and successors of the apostles received their commission and authority by the ritual of an imposition of hands (2 Tim 1:6). This was the sign of their reception of the grace necessary for the worthy fulfillment of their office. This does not mean, of course, that bishops and priests do not remain weak human beings. They remain very much so. Nevertheless, it is to them that Christ has entrusted the integrity of His word, His heart as the Good Shepherd, His body and His merciful forgiveness. The priests of the Church have borne this power through the centuries. They make it possible for everyone to encounter Christ and realize that He freely offers them the gift of salvation.

Among the apostles, St. Peter had been given a very special commission and the same applies to his successors. Jesus chose Peter to be that "rock" upon which He would build His Church. He made him the chief steward of His kingdom. It was to him that He promised that whatsoever he would bind on earth, it would be bound also in heaven, and whatsoever he would loose on earth, it would be loosed also in heaven (Mt 16:16–18). After the resurrection, Jesus entrusted to him the care of feeding his lambs and sheep (Jn 21:15–17). On the feast of Pentecost, it was Peter who acted as spokesman for the apostles and who first proclaimed the good news of Christ's resurrection (Acts 2:14–36). At the close of his zealous apostolic work, he suffered martyrdom in Rome. The commission of Peter must continue in the

Church, a solid rock-foundation holding together the entire edifice, participating in the strength of Christ and assuring the unity of the Church and the soundness of its faith until the end of time. The primitive Church held the firm conviction that the promise made to Peter and the authority given to him had not come to an end with his death. His successors in ministry and authority are the Roman Pontiffs, the bishops of that city in which Peter was the head of the Church in his last years.

Christ assists His emissaries in an efficacious way until the end of time. He is absolutely faithful to the new covenant He has made. We are thus assured that when a truth of faith is solemnly proclaimed by the whole body of the Church's bishops, together with the Pope as their head, such a dogma is infallibly true. This is not done, of course, on the basis of their own human power. It is done on the basis of the divine revelation which reaches its final stage in Jesus Christ. A solemn proclamation of this kind is actually a very rare occurrence. It takes place, most of the time, when it becomes absolutely necessary to prevent error from being accepted as truth. This infallibility of the Pope and the body of bishops united with him relates only to such truths as pertain to faith and morals. No infallibility is guaranteed them when it comes to questions of a scientific or political nature. A good Catholic listens with piety and love to what the Pope and the bishops have to say. Of greater importance, in a way, than these extraordinary proclamations, however, is the regular teaching (catechesis) of the bishops and priests, Sunday after Sunday, their regular direction of the spiritual life of the faithful. It is only human to expect that in fulfilling his ministry the defects and limitations of the priest will become apparent. In spite of this, however, what the priests, the pastors of the whole Church, proclaim with all their heart and soul to be the essence of the good news of the Lord still communicates to us, through the goodness of the Holy Spirit, the true word of Christ.

More than once in the past, and contrary to Christ's own

admonition, it has happened that Popes, bishops and priests have imitated the manners and the way of life of the rich and powerful of this world. We can be thankful to God that in our day divine providence and the grace of the Holy Spirit are leading the Church's representatives to take more and more to heart the words addressed to its priests by the very first Pope, St. Peter: "Tend the flock of God that is your charge, not by constraint but willingly, not for shameful gain but eagerly, not as domineering over those in your charge but being examples to the flock" (1 Pet 5:1-3). In these days, in most of the countries of the world, the acceptance of a call to the priesthood brings with it no material advantages or political power. It demands a readiness to shoulder the cross of Christ for the kingdom of God and its justice (Mt 6:33). The vocation of the priest today is not an easy one. Yet it is something worthy of giving one's whole life for. Those who feel they are being called by Christ should put their hands to the plow and not look back (Lk 9:62). They should push their plow into God's field. The Lord of the harvest will ripen their work with golden ears at the time of the harvest (Mt 9:38).

The Vocation of All Christians

To fulfill its mission the Church has an absolute need for the ministry of its priests. This in no way implies that other Christians have no role to play in the Church. Just the opposite. The entire household of God, as a people on pilgrimage toward an eternal home, participates on earth in the mission of Christ. The bishops and priests are commissioned to preach the Gospel by reason of their office. Any Christian, however, who has found the treasure of God's kingdom and experienced the joy of this discovery cannot refrain from speaking about his good fortune and sharing his joy with others. He knows well what a treasure is faith, which teaches us hope and confidence, and what a find is charity, freeing us, as it does, from imprisonment in our selfishness and creating new life in us and others as well. A single deed or word motivated sincerely by deep, living faith and love often has a greater impact on people than the most eloquent sermons heard in church. "You are the light of the world," Jesus said to all of His disciples. "Let your light shine before men" (Mt 5:14–16). No special training or knowledge is needed—simply faith, sincerity and unselfish love. How many children developed true faith seeing the hands of their fathers folded in prayer? How many children had genuine love implanted in their hearts by experiencing the unlimited goodness of their mothers? How many individuals have been disposed toward the grace of conversion because of the warm hearts of good friends?

In the Roman Empire, it was not so much because of the preaching of official missionaries that people began to be attracted to Christianity. It was more through the example of the lives of ordinary Christians with whom they came into daily contact that they embraced Christianity and caused it to spread like a brush fire. In that corrupt and aimless society, it became manifest that the persecuted Christians had some great treasure. They were ready to die for it, and it enabled them meanwhile to live with joy and hope. It was evident in that selfish, ambitious society that the Christians loved one another, came to one another's assistance, and did good even to those outside their fold. People realized that they entertained a hope that was stronger than any earthly power and failed to tremble even in the face of death. The ancient Roman burial places of the early Christians, the catacombs, with their primitive inscriptions, enable us to capture the sentiments of the faithful. "My dearest wife, Luciana, you are alive," reads one of the epitaphs. Such simple words, but what indomitable energy vibrates through them. A new world had come into being—a world of faith, hope, joy and peace.

What most effectively attracted the people of the Roman Empire to Christianity was, no doubt, the warm, brotherly love practiced by early Christians. "By this all men will know that you are my disciples, if you have love for one another," says St. John (Jn 13:35). The Acts of the Apostles, describing the Church in Jerusalem, says that "the company of those who believed were of one heart and soul." In our own day when, in a world more and more regulated by machines and the institutions of government, people increasingly feel themselves isolated from one another, it is essential for Christians to establish living communities. They must create communities in which the members know and respect one another, help one another and are ready to ask for and receive one another's forgiveness. The foundation of such communities cannot be simply human friendliness and natural good will. They have to be based on a firm belief in the fact that each individual is a child of the same God and that all are members of the one Christ, all sharing in the gifts of the same Holy Spirit.

These gifts of the Holy Spirit are manifold. God created human beings as individuals. The Holy Spirit guides all of them as distinct personalities. They are not all to be cast into the same mold. In God's garden there are flowers of every kind, from the humble daisy to the blood-red rose of Pentecost. All of them are dear to God. He loves them all and cares for all of them. The person whose heart is "attuned to the heart of God" feels the same way. It does not grieve him when he realizes people have natures, talents, interests and ways of thinking that are different from his own. He does not want to force his own opinion on others. He rejoices in the fact that people are so different because such variety reflects and expresses the inexhaustible richness of God's nature. His only concern is that differences not make for isolation, personalities not clash, special talents not be the source of pride, differences of ability and vocation not engender feelings of superiority and inferiority. St. Paul admonished his disciples in Thessalonica, "Do not quench the Spirit, but test everything; hold fast what is good" (1 Thess 5:19–21).

The good priest fosters the different activities of the faithful, tending every good shoot with loving care, alert to all the movements of the ever-renewing Holy Spirit. In the same way, the faithful should strive to bring it about that every member of the body of Christ benefits and develops through mutual service in relation to every other member, all in the spirit of unity, that the body of Christ may grow in love (Eph 4:16).

"That They All May Be One"

Jesus prayed for His disciples, "Holy Father, keep them in Thy name whom Thou has given Me, that they may be one, even as we are one" (Jn 17:11). "There is one Lord, one faith, one baptism, one God and Father of us all" (Eph 4:6). "By one Spirit we were all baptized into one body" (1 Cor 12:13). "Because there is one bread, we who are many are one body, for we all partake of the one bread" (1 Cor 10:17). All of these statements of St. Paul refer to the Church. The intention of Christ was for all the members of the Church, through one and the same God, one and the same Christ, one Holy Spirit, one faith, one baptism, one Eucharist, and by mutual love, to constitute a worldwide unity of one and the same Church of Jesus Christ. The original unity of the disciples of Christ, however, was eventually dissolved. The tragedy is that this was brought about through the sins of Christians themselves. During the first millennium of the Church's history, allowing for small regional schisms, the whole of Christianity constituted a single Church. Since the one Church had spread over the whole of the known world of the time, it came to be called "Catholic," the Greek term for "universal." In the eleventh century, however, a split occurred between the Eastern (Greek) and the Western (Latin) Church. The causes of the split were mainly of a cultural and political nature, but the schism has not yet been healed. Later, in the sixteenth century, the movement called the Reformation swept across Europe. The Reformation had its source in the widespread corruption of the Church in the Middle Ages and the Renaissance.

The zeal of the Reformers led to extremes. Even certain matters that pertain to the very essence of Catholic teaching came to be rejected, for example, the role of bishops and priests, the primacy of the Pope, confession, and the sacrifice of the Mass. The Reformation ended in another schism within the Church. Several Protestant churches sprang up in opposition to the Catholic Church. These churches, in turn, eventually split up among themselves.

It is pointless today to attempt to assess the responsibility and blame for these lamentable events. Many mistakes had been made on all sides. One thing, however, is very important to keep in mind. It is unjust to hold today's Christians responsible for the mistakes of the past. For this reason, a good Catholic today does not view as an enemy or a competitor a Christian who, through no fault of his, has been baptized and obtained his knowledge of Christ in a Protestant church, who reads the Bible and strives with faith, hope and love to live the life of a true Christian. Such a person a good Catholic views as a true and beloved brother in Christ. It is true that from the Catholic viewpoint Protestant teachings, organization and worship leave certain things to be desired. But there is much more that binds Catholics and Protestants together. And these things are of greater importance than those which divide us. Our Protestant brothers and sisters believe in Jesus Christ, just as we do. They try, as we do, to walk in His footsteps. In the light of such considerations, through the inspiration of the Holy Spirit, the Church today is endeavoring to heal the wounds of separation, so that all Christians may once again become one, in accordance with the intention of Christ. Christian unity cannot be realized, of course, through compromises. It can be brought about only when the different Christian groups come together in the spirit of mutual love and try to realize the Gospel of Christ in the most faithful manner. We can be thankful to God that it is the Gospel of Christ that is our common source. When Christians are prepared to follow the inspiration of the Holy Spirit with unselfish dedication, they gradually will move closer to one another. One day they will experience the fact that the sunlight of truth and the warm breeze of charity has melted the icebergs erected between them because of prejudice, stubbornness, misunderstanding, anger, bitterness and indifference. In this way the body of Christ, the Church, will increasingly grow toward its proper fulfillment.

The inexhaustible source of unity and growth in the Church is its worship. In the liturgy, the whole Christian community, by the strength of the Holy Spirit, carries on the prayer of Christ till the end of the world. The center of this liturgy or worship is to be found in the sacraments, and above all in the Mass.

REFLECTION AND DISCUSSION

1. Is my Christian faith a hazy belief? An abstract theory? A shaky opinion? Or is it a full, trusting commitment to the living God, the God who has declared His love for me in Jesus Christ?

2. What is the core of Christian faith? Can I express it in my own words in a single sentence? What would I answer to people who might ask me, "Why do you believe in Jesus Christ?"

3. Read 1 Cor 13 and substitute the name "Jesus" for the word "love." See if it fits. What is the connection between God's love and ours? How can Christlike love become concrete in our daily relations in the family, the school, the office, the factory,

the life of the nation and international affairs? Read 1 Jn 3:11–18 and 4:7–12 and ask yourself if you have fully accepted the teaching contained in these passages and have genuinely tried to live according to it.

4. What do I hope for? Am I hoping to get something, or am I hoping to be? What does "to be" really mean?

5. How do I think about the Church? As an outsider criticizing it? As a customer utilizing its services? As a member of the family, who loves it and feels himself responsible for it? Do I feel a bond of solidarity with all my Christian brothers and sisters throughout the world?

6. What do I think is the main task of the Christian Church today? Does the local congregation to which I belong actually appear to be a concretization of the one universal Church of Jesus Christ? Is the congregation really united? How could it become more united? Is it a holy congregation? How could it become more holy? Is it serving society, representing the love of Christ, who came to serve, in its mission to society?

7. Do I treasure Holy Scripture and the apostolic tradition handed down to us through generations of believers? Do I feel responsible for handing them down to the next generation? Is Scripture my favorite reading? If not, why is this so? Do I look to the Bible for guidance in my choices? How can I find in the great variety contained in the Bible the core and kernel that sheds light on all the rest?

8. What is my attitude toward those who are now carrying on the commission given by Christ to His apostles, i.e., the Pope, bishops and priests of the Church? Do I make a genuine effort to hear the voice of Christ being transmitted to me

through them? Is Christ calling me, perhaps, to offer my life to His exclusive service by joining the ranks of those who will carry on the apostolic commission until the end of the world?

9. Is my faith a source of joy and something I want to share with others, so that we might rejoice in it together? Are my faith and my love contagious?

10. Am I concerned to be obedient to the wish expressed in Christ's prayer: "Father, keep them, so that they may be one" (Jn 17:11)? Am I praying, suffering and working for the unity of all Christians in truth and love, or am I really persisting in building walls of separation?

Chapter 3

"The Fountains of Living Water"

The Sacraments

What, actually, is the nature of the sacraments?

St. John's Gospel tells us that on the occasion of the great Jewish feast day—"on the last day of the feast, the great day" (Jn 7:37)—Jesus exclaimed, "If anyone thirst, let him come to Me. Let him drink who believes in Me. As Scripture has said, 'Out of his heart shall flow rivers of living water'" (Jn 7:37–38). St. John's own commentary on these words of Jesus reads as follows: "Now this He said about the Spirit, which those who believed in Him were to receive" (Jn 7:39). The "living water" is the Spirit, and Jesus, through His death and resurrection, will give this Spirit to those who believe in Him. Jesus Himself, the heart of Jesus, is the fountain of this living water (cf. Jn 19:34; 4:14). In the Incarnate Son of God, Jesus Christ, God's forgiving and life-giving love took on human form. Those who encountered Jesus encountered this divine love. To those who received forgiveness from Jesus God granted forgiveness. When Jesus touched the sick or the dead, it was actually God's life-giving power that had touched them. Thus the encounter with Jesus became for those living in His day the visible sign of God's grace and love, a face mediating God's action in a human experience.

After His resurrection, Jesus returned to His Father. But He is still with us, although we who are not yet sharing the full glory and effects of His resurrection are unable to encounter Him in a visible, audible, experimental way. He is invisible to us. Nevertheless, our encounter with Him is absolutely essential if we are to come into contact with God's love. Jesus found a way, therefore, for this tangible, experimental way of encountering Him to become possible, a way in keeping with His new, resurrected being. He speaks to us in the words He entrusted to His apostles. He is present to us in the Scriptures. His role of mediating grace becomes tangible to us in the Church as a whole. He wanted to render this encounter with Him more immediate for us, however, through the most important life-giving functions of the Church. These life-giving actions of the Church are the sacraments. The Catholic Church treasures seven such sacraments as precious gifts of Christ. In each one of them there is to be found a symbolic action as an essential ingredient. We are washed, a hand touches us on the forehead, we share a common meal. These are ancient symbols that can also be found in other religions. In the Christian ritual, however, there is always the utterance of a word either grounded in or directly derived from the Gospel. This word gives a special meaning to the ritual, determines the meaning of the action, refers it to the saving action of Christ, creating a special relationship between this action and the saving deed of Christ. These rituals, therefore, are not just human cultic actions. In these actions it is the risen Christ Himself who comes to meet us, the fountain of the living waters, the Holy Spirit. It is in and through the sacraments that Christ continues His work. In the sacraments, Christ gathers together the scattered children of God. He unites them to Himself and thus opens for them the way to the Father (Eph 2:18).

It is in the name of Jesus that the ministers of the Church dispense the sacraments to us. In the sacraments the life of Jesus is generated and nourished within us. In and through them, Jesus gives us His Spirit, the Spirit that enables us to live a life of faith, hope and charity. The sacraments do not produce their effects mechanically, however. In His dealings with us, God does not force anyone. It is up to the human being to respond to God's call. It is through the profound meaning of the sacramental rituals that God calls us. Over the centuries, the Church, in its maternal care, has wonderfully elaborated upon these rituals. It is ever renewing them with the intention of rendering them ever more beautiful and meaningful. By the power of the Holy Spirit, God thus calls to us in the depths of our being, inviting us to participate in a Christ-like manner of life. But it is up to each one of us to respond. Nobody can answer in our place. When a little baby experiences a mother's caressing smile, a current of love reaches its very heart, and the baby at last returns the smile. The smile is assuredly the smile of the baby. At the same time, however, it is the result of the mother's unbounded love. Without maternal love, there will be no smile on the baby's face. And it is a remarkable fact that the person who is made the happiest by the infant's smile is the very mother who caused it to appear on the baby's face. So it is with us and God. Perhaps that is why it is said that the heart of a mother is the window through which we see the heart of God.

When a person follows the call of Christ and approaches the sacraments, he is making an external profession of his faith (Rom 10:9–10). Receiving a sacrament without interior faith, merely for the sake of external conformity or in a spirit of hypocrisy, contributes nothing toward our salvation. The whole of the New Testament stresses that the foundation of salvation is faith. Once a man possesses faith, he abandons a position of pride and conceit and relies on God's loving forgiveness. His heart is then opened up to receive the grace of divine sonship. The individual and the Church as a whole express and deepen their faith through the sacraments. It is our manner of adoration and a sure means of obtaining the renewed strength we need to lead a Christ-like way of life.

Baptism

The first of the seven sacraments is baptism. Jesus Himself originated this sacrament after His resurrection. "Go, therefore," He said, "and make disciples of all nations, baptizing them in the name of the Father and of the Son and of the Holy Spirit" (Mt 28:19). In keeping with the command of Jesus, the priest or his substitute bathes us with water by pouring it on our head as he says the words, "I baptize you (here inserting our baptismal name) in the name of the Father and of the Son and of the Holy Spirit." This symbol clearly expresses the essential meaning of baptism. In baptism, in and through Jesus and the Holy Spirit, God the Father cleanses us from our sins (Acts 2:38). From the very beginning a flood of sin has flowed through the course of human history. The Bible relates how the first human beings fell into sin, and this downward trend has engulfed all humanity (original sin). Since that fall, humanity has become geared, as it were, to commit personal sins unless a superior power restrains it. This superior power is God's Holy Spirit. The fundamental grace of baptism is the outpouring of the Holy Spirit into our hearts, becoming in the utmost depths of our soul the perennial fountain of faith and love (Jn 3:5; Tit 3:5). This Spirit of divine sonship is possessed only by those who have become one with Christ, the only-begotten Son of God. It is baptism that unites us with Christ (Gal 3:27). It immerses us into His death and resurrection (Rom 6:3–5; Col 2:12). The Holy Spirit is the life-giving Spirit of the Church, the head of which is Christ. Baptism makes us members of the Church and enables us to enjoy the prerogatives and take on the duties of disciples of Christ.

Baptism represents a decisive moment in a person's life. In baptism we are reborn as a child of God. We become a member of the body of Christ. We are made holy, living temples of the Holy Spirit. In baptism we are delivered "from the dominion of darkness and transferred to the kingdom of His beloved Son"

(Col 1:13). We reject Satan and all his temptations. We confess our belief in God our Savior. Later on, during the Mass of the Vigil on every Holy Saturday night, it is the custom for the faithful to renew their baptismal promises in preparation for the feast of Easter.

At baptism the community of the faithful receives the new member as a brother or a sister invited to the table of the Lord. It is an unforgettable event. This is particularly true in missionary countries, where the greater number of the faithful finds Christ in adulthood and they are baptized into the Church as adults.

It is true, of course, that by the mysterious operation of God's grace, conversion and salvation are possible for those who through no fault of their own cannot receive the sacrament of baptism. God has willed, however, that the ordinary way to salvation is to be by way of a person's entering into His household through baptism and, as a co-worker of Christ, contributing to the salvation of all and the building of God's kingdom in this world by his life, example, words and prayer.

Since baptism is so essential, it is an ancient custom in the Church for Christian parents to have their children baptized shortly after birth. Naturally, the infant is not yet in a position to believe, hope and love. Just as God's grace precedes an individual's response in the case of an adult, however, in the same way God fills the soul of the baptized infant with His sanctifying grace. This grace is asked for the child in the name of the faith of the whole Church. It remains true, of course, that when the child reaches the use of reason he has to commit himself to faith, hope and charity through a personal choice. That is why the Church baptizes only those children whose Christian upbringing is assured. When the growing child hears the good news of Jesus Christ through the voice of his parents, godparents, teachers and priests, the Holy Spirit, who is already dwelling in his heart by the grace of baptism, enables him to believe, understand and follow Christian teaching. Jesus draws this child toward Himself just the way He drew the children of Galilee to Himself when they crowded around Him. He took one of them and embraced him, uttering those memorable words, "Truly, I say to you, unless you turn and become like children, you will never enter the kingdom of heaven" (Mt 18:2–3).

The divine life becomes a reality within us when God, because of Jesus, His only-begotten Son, the risen Christ, forgives our sins, makes us members of His Son's body and gives us His Spirit and that of His Son, to become in us the source of faith and love. This threefold reality constitutes an indivisible unity. That is why baptism, confirmation and the Holy Eucharist are so closely related to one another. The special effect of baptism, as we have seen, is the washing away of our sins. That of confirmation is an outpouring of the Holy Spirit within us. The fruit of the Eucharist is a personal union between us and Christ. Because of the unity of the divine life a sacrament received earlier anticipates in some way the fruits of those received later. Thus baptism gives us the Holy Spirit and unites us with Christ.

Confirmation

Confirmation is the sacrament which expressly unites us in a living way with the Holy Spirit. It is administered by the bishop or, by special authorization, by a priest. The bishop places his hand on our head, anoints our forehead with holy oil and prays that the Holy Spirit be given to us. Both the laying on of hands and the anointing with oil express the fact that the believer shares in the strength of the Holy Spirit and thus receives a special commission. It is as though the hand of Christ were resting on our heads, as He tells us, "Go, love as I have loved. Be a witness of the fact that God is love." The oil is a sign of our participation in the mission of Christ. "The unction" which "anointed" Jesus as the Christ was no earthly ointment, but the Holy Spirit Himself. Jesus applies the words of the prophet Isaiah to Himself, "The Spirit of the Lord is upon Me, because He has anointed Me to preach good news to the poor" (Lk 4:18). It is by the Holy Spirit that we also become witnesses of the Gospel of Christ. Our faith and patience, our love and inner spiritual joy are testimony to the fact that Christ has actually redeemed the world.

The Eucharist, the Sacrament of the Altar

At the Last Supper Jesus took bread and a cup of wine into His hands. He declared the bread and wine His own sacrificed body and blood, distributed them among His disciples and commanded them: "Do this in memory of Me." For two thousand years the Church has faithfully carried out this command of Christ. Everywhere, in the branch-covered chapels of the jungles of Africa, the ice-covered churches of frozen Alaska, the magnificent cathedrals of Rome, Cologne and Paris, the prayer-hovels of the Andes, day in and day out, Christ's priests repeat, over 400,000 times, the words of Christ at the Last Supper. Millions upon millions share in the body and blood of the Lord. St. Paul calls this event "the Lord's Supper" (1 Cor 11:20). Ever since the Middle Ages Catholics have called it "the Mass," taken from the Latin word, "missa." It is the center and source of the Christian life. In the Mass, out of the warmth of His heart, Jesus has left us His greatest gift. With the omnipotent divine word uttered by the priest who follows in His footsteps and exercises the authority He has granted him, Jesus transforms the essence of bread and wine into His own body and blood. He transforms them into Himself for our nourishment, identifying His sacrifice of life with our life. It is true that our eyes perceive only bread and wine upon the altar. Our faith, however, believing unconditionally in the truth of the words of Christ, enables us to understand that this is now the very Lord who died for us and rose again from the dead. Just as ordinary food nourishes our life at the price of ceasing to be itself for the sake of another, so Jesus

here gives His life for us. He has lived and died for us. Now He
gives us Himself as food and drink so that we may be completely
united with Him and, in Him, with one another. Ordinary bread
becomes transformed into the body of the one who eats it. This
"sacred" bread, coming down from heaven, transforms into itself the one who receives it with faith and love.

Through the power of the Holy Spirit, it is Jesus Himself
who is present among us under the appearances of bread and
wine, which signify His life-giving death. He draws us to Himself
and makes us partakers of His death and resurrection. The
words of Jesus clearly tell us that the bread, that is, what we now
see as bread, is "His body given up for us," and what we now
see as wine is His "blood shed for us." But these signs are not
signs of an endless death. The bread and wine are food and
drink and therefore sources of life. It is in the Mass that the
Church recalls this holy mystery and gives thanks for it, the very
word "Eucharist" meaning "the giving of thanks." Naturally, the
risen, glorified body of the Lord can die no more. In the Mass,
however, the one sacrifice of Jesus becomes our sacrifice, enabling us to share abundantly in the fruits of the redemption.
The whole Church, and not just those who are present at Mass,
receives these abundant fruits, especially those who are remem-
bered. At the time of Holy Communion in the Mass Jesus comes
to us. He desires the tiny rivers of our lives to merge into the sea
of His divine life, so that He may truly remain in us forever (Jn
6:56). "As the living Father sent Me, and I live because of the
Father, so he who eats Me will live because of Me" (Jn 6:57).

In the early Church, right from the beginning, it was the
custom for the faithful to gather together for the Eucharist on
Sunday, the day of the Lord's resurrection, and to receive the
body and blood of the Lord. Later on, the Church made presence at Sunday Mass and reception of the Lord's body at Easter-
time matters of obligation. This is hardly a burdensome
obligation, however, for the Christian who understands the

meaning of his faith and the great value of the grace of Christ. Rather, he considers it a prerogative, a privilege to be treasured. He will endeavor to participate as often as he can in this banquet of the family of Christ. It is the Lord Himself who invites His brothers and sisters. He gives Himself to us as the food of eternal life. "He who eats My flesh and drinks My blood has eternal life, and I will raise him up at the last day" (Jn 6:54).

The Sacrament of Reconciliation

The sacrament of reconciliation is Jesus' Easter gift to us. On the evening of the first Easter, Jesus said to His disciples: "Receive the Holy Spirit. Whose sins you shall forgive, they are forgiven them; whose sins you shall retain they are retained" (Jn 20:23).

Love has not yet permeated every particle of our hearts and souls—far from it. There is no individual who can say he has not sinned in thought, word, deed and omission, when we confess in common our sins and shortcomings at the beginning of every Mass. St. James reminds us that "we all make many mistakes" (Jas 3:2). Unless a person radically rejects God's love, however, his sins do not erase the grace of divine sonship from his heart. In this case, the sins, in traditional terminology, are called "venial sins," and there is no one who is totally free from them. But there are certain thoughts, words, deeds and omissions which constitute, with complete knowledge, a flat rejection of the will of God. These sins are in total opposition to the love of God and our fellow man. In such cases a person radically rejects the good and chooses with complete understanding—for some apparent advantage—something which is very evil. He thus commits a "mortal sin." This does not happen easily in the life of a person who takes his Christian faith seriously. It surely is not a common occurrence of everyday life. But human beings are so weak that such an unfortunate thing can happen. The words of St. Paul addressed to the Corinthians who took certain sins too lightly apply in such a case: "Do not be deceived. Do you not know that the unrighteous will not inherit the kingdom of God?" (1 Cor 6:9).

Is all hope lost, therefore, for such unfortunate sinners? Thanks be to God, no. There is no limit to God's mercy. The love of Christ knows no bounds. He is still calling, still waiting, still looking for the lost sheep. In order to be forgiven again, however, it is absolutely necessary for such a sinner to repent with heartfelt sincerity and to make amends, as far as he can, for the harm he may have caused, to confess his sins to a priest, as a representative of the Church, and to ask forgiveness of the priest by the power given him by Christ for this purpose. Once he has obtained forgiveness he will be allowed to approach the table of the Lord as a full-fledged member of the Church. His heart will come alive again with the love that is expressed in and through the banquet of the Lord.

Strictly speaking, we are obliged to have recourse to the sacrament of reconciliation only when we are conscious of unconfessed mortal sin. It is very advisable, however, to make use of this sacrament as also a very effective means to combat our other sins. The good advice obtained from our confessor can be very helpful to us. An individual is in a seriously dangerous state of mind if he gets to the point of persuading himself that what is in reality evil is good for him, that sinning is natural, that lukewarmness is common sense and indifference is prudence. It is extremely important to understand that evil is evil! It remains evil even when it is committed by me. It is evil, indeed, but it also can be forgiven.

The confessional remains the only place today where people do not parade their virtues or make excuses, but confess the wrong they have done. In this way they prove that they look at it as something incompatible with their Christian vocation and something they would like to get rid of. A good confession is an encounter with Christ, the merciful and compassionate Redeemer. It is a source of true joy. We are forgiven, washed clean again. We can once more set out on the path of following in the footsteps of the Lord. One thing we should never forget, however, and that is the fact that in order to obtain God's forgiveness for ourselves, we must show forgiveness toward one another. Jesus stressed again and again, "If you forgive men their trespasses, your heavenly Father also will forgive you; but if you do not forgive men their trespasses, neither will your Father forgive you your trespasses" (Mt 6:14–15). The condition and, at the same time, the effect of our reconciliation with God is our reconciliation with others, forgiving them even as often as "seventy times seven" (Mt 18:22). Only those who know how much in need of God's forgiveness they themselves are can be forgiving of others. Only those who pray daily, "Forgive us our trespasses," can truly forgive those who have trespassed against them.

The Sacrament of the Sick

There is another sacrament similar to the sacrament of reconciliation. It is known as extreme unction, or, better, the sacrament of the anointing of the sick. St. James refers to this sacrament when he writes, "Is any among you sick? Let him call for the elders of the Church, and let them pray over him, anointing him with oil in the name of the Lord. And the prayer of faith will save the sick man, and the Lord will raise him up; and if he has committed sins, he will be forgiven" (Jas 5:14–15).

In this sacrament Christ helps his sick brothers and sisters to carry their cross of sickness in union with His own. By the power of His resurrection He enables them to overcome the temptations of dejection, fear and vacillation of faith occasioned by their sickness, and He leads them safely in the direction of eternal life. If God wills it, this sacrament sometimes helps to restore the sick person to health. On this ground alone, therefore, it is not correct to look upon it as a sacrament only for those on the threshold of death. That is why the Church in our day no longer calls it the sacrament of extreme unction, but the sacrament of the sick. The elderly, even if they are healthy, are allowed to receive this sacrament, since in the regular sequence of events death is not far off for them. Even when health is not restored, this sacrament helps the sick to accept their sufferings in the joy and peace of Christ, enabling them to unite their sufferings with the redemptive suffering of the Lord. The sick person can make the words of St. Paul his own: "Now I rejoice in my sufferings for your sake, and in my flesh I complete what is lacking in Christ's afflictions for the sake of His body, that is, the Church" (Col 1:24). What is still "lacking" is not on the part of Christ, but on our part. Once we accept our part in the spirit of Christ, then the cross of Christ becomes all-embracing and will be fulfilled in the resurrection.

Holy Orders

There are two sacraments that enable human beings to undertake a special vocation in life. One of them is the sacrament whereby bishops are consecrated and priests ordained. As we mentioned earlier, it was through the imposition of the hands of a bishop accompanied by the appropriate prayers that Christ accepted new members in the fellowship of His apostles, enabling them to take part in the vocation of the apostles to preach, lead the various communities of the Church, offer the Mass and administer the other sacraments, strengthening them with the graces necessary for the faithful fulfillment of all these duties.

Matrimony

The second sacrament of this nature is the sacrament of matrimony. In this sacrament Christ grants the help a married couple needs to live in such a way that faith and love will be realized in a practical way in their married life. Pledging themselves to each other, "until death do us part," it will not be possible for them to keep that pledge faithfully for an entire lifetime unless God Himself becomes a partner in their marriage. He will never abandon the married couple that puts its trust in Him. He will assist the married pair through the power of His grace to enable the love they bear for each other to grow into a likeness of the love with which Christ loves His Church (Eph 5:25–33).

The sacrament of matrimony is actualized by the symbolic act of the bride and groom when each of them responds, "Yes, I will," to the other. By their mutual consent they mediate the grace of Christ to each other. This grace will enable them to realize their love for Christ through their love for each other and for their children. Such a married life is based on mutual love and daily prayer in common. It is a life full of sacrifice, yet a happy one all the same because it is rooted in unbounded confidence in God and each other. Such a family is a living cell of the Church, its smallest yet most important unit.

A Life with God, a Life with Our Fellow Men

The seven sacraments are the seven fountains of living waters! They are the actions of Christ through which He reaches out and draws all human beings to Himself, making it possible for them to follow in His footsteps on the path of love toward God and fellow human beings. If anyone regularly frequents the sacraments and does not manifest genuinely from his heart a love for his fellow men in speech and action, making no effort to follow in the footsteps of Christ, he should consider himself a liar and a hypocrite. St. John writes: "If anyone says, 'I love God,' and hates his brother, he is a liar; for he who does not love his brother whom he has seen, cannot love God whom he has not seen" (1 Jn 4:20). How can he love God if another human being, who is so important to God, has no significance for him? The sacraments are sources of grace, but they impart to us a mission at the same time. Every divine gift entails a mission along with it.

A life nourished by the sacraments is a life in which love for God and man are inseparably united.

Life with God means a life of prayer. Christ prayed very often. He taught us the lesson that when we pray we are not to multiply well-chosen words, but are to address God with the simplicity with which a child speaks to his loving Father ("Our Father"—Mt 6:9). There is no need to talk at length about all our needs (Mt 6:7–8, 32). Jesus did not draw the conclusion from this, however, that prayer is superfluous. Just the opposite. We are admonished to pray always (Lk 18:1).

In prayer, sometimes we give praise to God. At other times, we give Him thanks. Again, we ask Him for something, because we are always in need of His assistance. A true prayer of petition, however, never pressures God or sets limits for Him. Instead, the petition is left in the hands of God: "Thy will be done."

It is an ancient custom for Christian people to pray both in the morning and again at night. This provides a framework and a goal for our life. We must be careful, however, that this practice not become sheer routine. It is impossible to overestimate the importance of family prayer in common, particularly at the end of the day. These brief moments of prayer, however, are only the beginning of a deeper penetration into the great and profound world of prayer. Only those whose minds are ever alert, in loving awareness and faith in God, to the fact that God is always present and caring for us have really reached the mysterious depths of this world. It is then the most natural attitude for us to be with Him and to be mindful of Him. Once the awareness of the presence of God becomes almost second nature to us, our hearts expand to include all our fellow human beings within them.

The Christian life is also, therefore, a life with and for our fellow human beings. We do not live for ourselves, but for others: husband for wife and wife for husband; parents for their children; doctors for their patients; all of us for our fellow human beings, cooperating to build a better world, a human society based on justice and love. With reference to everyone, it is true, but most of all with respect to those who suffer, who are poor and oppressed, our Lord said, speaking about the last judgment, "Truly I say to you, as you did it to one of the least of these My brethren, you did it to Me" (Mt 25:40). What we do for ourselves, we do for ourselves, and that is all there is to it. But what we do for others for the sake of Christ is done to Christ, and in so acting we are sowing the seeds of something eternal. The Second Vatican Council reminds us that love and the fruits of love endure forever (*Gaudium et Spes*, The Church in the Modern World, n. 39). And that is our hope.

REFLECTION AND DISCUSSION

1. Are the sacraments for me a genuine faith-encounter with the living Christ, or do I approach them as customs and in a routine fashion?

2. Do I appreciate the fact of having been baptized as being a sign of God's prevenient grace? Are the light of my baptismal candle and the whiteness of my baptismal robe still shining in my soul? Do the words of St. Paul, "You are the children of light" (Eph 5:8), really apply to me? What would I answer if I were asked who I was? Would I reply, "I am the child of God the Father, a member of the body of Christ, the temple of God's Holy Spirit," or are certain purely human relationships more important to me in terms of my identity?

3. What kind of "firmness" or "strength" is it that is bestowed on us in confirmation? How did Jesus conceive

"strength"? Is this conception very different from the way we usually think of it?

4. Is it a privilege or a burden for me to attend Mass? The Mass is variously called "the Lord's supper," "the sacrifice of the new covenant," "the paschal meal of Christ's disciples," "partaking in the living bread which came down from heaven," and "the source and peak of the whole life of the Church." What does each of these expressions mean? How are they related to one another? In what ways is the living Christ present among us? What did the Lord's supper mean for St. Paul (1 Cor 10 and 11)? What did it mean for St. John (Jn 6)?

5. Have I the honesty and the courage to acknowledge my faults and ask for the forgiveness of God and the Church? Or do I try to excuse myself and accuse others? Are my confessions a childish formality or a real encounter with God's mercy in Christ? Am I ready to forgive people "seventy times seven times," or do I set limits to my forgiveness? Do I realize that human relations cannot be ordered on the basis of justice alone, that justice has to be enveloped by mercy? Since mercy without justice and justice without mercy are equally insufficient, how can we build a human society that will be built on both justice *and* mercy? What can I do about it?

6. Do I consider or live the married life as a concretization of Christlike love, founded on faith? Do the words of Christ, "Where two or three come together in my name, I am there with them" (Mt 18:20), apply to my own family? Does my behavior help all the members of my family to experience the presence of Christ in their midst?

7. Is prayer for me just as natural as breathing? Do I feel the urge, as Jesus did, to devote a part of my time to prayer? Am

I capable of listening to the "sounds of silence," or do I always need some noise to fill my emptiness? Is my prayer a mechanical routine, or does it grow organically with me? How many of my actions are performed just for myself, and how many of them are done for God, for Christ, for my fellow human beings?

Chapter 4

"I Live and You Will Live Also"

There Is a Future Life

"I live, and you will live also" (Jn 14:19). These confident words spoken by Jesus as He set out on His way toward death express in a marvelous way the essence of Christian hope. There is no power so terrible as the death that awaits all living creatures. There is no escaping it for plants, animals and human beings alike. According to modern science there will come a day when all life will have vanished from the earth. The whole human race and all its earthly achievements will be shrouded in death.

But the heart of man longs for eternal life. For a loving heart, the thought is too much to bear that one's father or mother, one's husband or wife, one's child or one's friend will disappear without a trace, will have become but dust and ashes. Their loving eyes revealed such wondrous depths, their hearts were aflame with such goodness, their very existence was so meaningful, irreplaceable, unique. It would be an unbearable thought for human beings to believe that everything they have accomplished will be eaten away by rust, covered with dust and broken to bits by decay, that the entire human race on which so much labor and sacrifice has been spent through the centuries will be reduced to nothingness, like a tiny curl of a wave which disappears the moment the wind subsides. Is the future awaiting us, then,

72

nothing but swirling atoms? Even if we assume that life might begin again on other planets in some other solar system, would it be of any avail if they, in turn, were destined to collapse into chaos, and the whole meaningless circle were to be traced over and over again without end? Evolution without a goal is just as meaningless as a road that leads nowhere. Man's heart cannot be satisfied with a prospect such as this, which deprives everything of its meaning. Yet the reign of death would make it appear as if this were indeed the prospect we would have to envision.

It is at just this point, however, that the voice of Christ thunders into the history of mankind: "I live, and you will live also." God created the world not for death, but for life. Death is only a station on the way to future life. At the end of our earthly pilgrimage God is waiting for us, just as He stood there at its beginning and has been accompanying His creatures along the path of their pilgrimage. He is the First and the Last, the Beginning and the End, the Alpha and the Omega. He is the fountain of life, giving life to all. Through the mission of the Son and the Holy Spirit He is already nourishing a life in human beings which will endure forever. Jesus declared: "He who believes in Me, though he die, yet shall he live; and whoever lives and believes in Me shall never die" (Jn 11:25–26). "He who believes in Me," he who follows in My footsteps, he in whom My own heart beats, He is saying, will remain alive with Me, in Me, through Me; he will live with My risen life, no matter that one day his heart will stop and his body will return to dust. "I am the resurrection and the life. . . . I will raise him up on the last day" (Jn 11:25; 6:54). This is the Gospel, the "good news" of Jesus. Just as He asked His friend Martha, so now He is asking us, "Do you believe this?" (Jn 11:26). And millions of Christians answer Him: "Yes, Lord, we believe that You are the resurrection, You are the life. He who believes in You shall not perish forever."

We Shall Rise Again

When Jesus spoke of eternal life to come, He used the word "resurrection." That is why, in the Apostles' Creed, we say, "We believe in the resurrection of the body." It has already been pointed out that the risen body will be radically different from the body in its present state. It will no longer be subject to the limitations of time and space, but will share in the freedom of the Holy Spirit. We still call it a body because, just as our earthly body is an expression of our soul and the instrument through which we communicate with one another, so in the world to come will there be a human community, in which we will know one another, be happy together and praise the goodness of God in common. Of course, "no eye has seen, nor ear heard, nor the heart of man conceived, what God has prepared for those who love Him" (1 Cor 2:9). If one sees only the tiny, hard, brown cherry seed, how can he imagine the wondrous cherry tree, with its majestic snow-white blossoms, that will spring from it? If one sees only the hairy caterpillar crawling lazily upon the ground, how can he imagine the butterfly with rainbow-colored wings that will develop from it? All the more is it impossible for us, before experiencing it, to picture to ourselves the beauty and happiness of that land the Father has prepared for those upon whom He has shed His grace from the beginning of the world (Mt 25:35). Perhaps we can catch a brief glimpse of that other world in the look of wonder in the eyes and the smile on the face of a holy Christian who is taking leave of this life. Although we have no way of imagining our heavenly abode, still it gives meaning to our entire life. Because we know there is such a "home" which Jesus went before us to prepare (Jn 14:2), there is a real meaning given to our earthly pilgrimage. Because there is a heavenly barn in which to store the fruits of God's harvest (Mt 13:30), there is real meaning in the labor of those who sow and reap. Nothing will be lost that the Holy Spirit has enlivened.

Since the heart of Jesus, the center of every heart, is stronger than death, everything that love accomplishes lives for all eternity.

Life or Death?

This is our unwavering hope. At the same time, however, it serves as a reminder to all mankind. Where there is love in the spirit of the love of Christ, there also is eternal life. But where love does not prevail, death has already made its entrance. Unless there is repentance, this spells eternal death, eternal damnation. Man is not simply a product of the inevitable laws of nature. He is a creature endowed with intelligence, capable of molding himself through his free decisions. It is of the very essence of his nature to be able to know the truth and to choose the good with freedom, thus forming his own being in a creative way. If he strives sincerely to know the truth and make it his own, if he is willing to choose the good and to live by it, then he becomes a human being made in the image and likeness of God. If, on the other hand, he seeks only his self-interest rather than the truth, if he simply pursues his own advantage instead of doing what is good, he places himself in contradiction to his own deepest destiny and destroys in himself the image of the God of truth and goodness.

The teaching of Christ, His example, His life, death and resurrection, the coming of the Holy Spirit, His action, His divine grace—all these have only one goal and that is for man to arrive, through faith and love, at a knowledge of the truth (1 Tim 2:4) and to realize the good. God does not use force, however, in dealing with man. Love cannot be forced. Faith and love are the result of a man's fundamental choice. This choice takes place in the deepest layer of our soul, a layer of which we ourselves are hardly aware. Yet the whole human life is determined by this choice: either love, freedom and God, or self-interest, passion and pride. It often seems in this earthly life of ours that those who have chosen to live a good life come to grief, while those who are cunning, domineering and unscrupulous succeed. But this is only the outward appearance of things. For there is a God.

Man's existence does not end with death. Once he has died, he has reached a state in which it will no longer be possible for him to change his basic attitude. He will forever remain what he has made of himself in his earthly life: either the loving child of the Father, in union with the Son and the Holy Spirit, or the petrified contradiction of a totally isolated self-centeredness. This latter state is called hell: a human being who can be happy only with love, only with God, rejects love and God forever and thus, by his own choice, becomes the victim of his own eternal unhappiness. Jesus, "the way, the truth and the life" (Jn 14:6), has warned us again and again of this danger (Mt 24:36–51). He underwent a sorrowful death for us precisely in order to set before our eyes, and save us from, the dreadful, destructive power of sin.

Our Hope

The thought of eternal damnation can fill us with terror. Jesus Himself admonishes us to "fear him who can destroy both body and soul in hell" (Mt 10:28). Yet the lives of millions of Christians over the past two thousand years testify to the fact that the fundamental Christian feeling is not one of fear, but of joy, gratitude and hope. St. Paul exclaims: "If God is for us, who is against us?" "Who shall separate us from the love of Christ?" (Rom 8:31–39). St. John tells us, "There is no fear in love, but perfect love casts out fear" (1 Jn 4:18–19).

Jesus left us peace—His peace (Jn 14:27). He gave us joy—His joy (Jn 16:22). No one can take them from us. We are already on the way to God. We are already His household, already seated at His table. We are even now living with His life. With the eyes of faith, even now we are seeing with His eyes. We embrace the world with His heart, the heart of love. "It is no longer I who live, but Christ who lives in me" (Gal 2:20). God lives in us and we in Him, both now and forever. It is true that we often experience the wavering of our faith and hope, and our love is often tepid. But we know that God is our loving Father, "who [having begun] a good work in [us] will bring it to completion at the day of Jesus Christ" (Phil 1:6), on the final judgment day. Often when the moment of death comes this good work is not yet brought to completion. There has to be a "place" of purification, therefore. We call it a place, but it is rather a process or a state in which God cleanses our hearts of the dross of which we were not able to rid ourselves during our earthly life. The essential happiness of heaven is love. The individual who has not made love the very center of his life is not fully prepared to enjoy heaven to the full, to feel at home and at ease there. His heart has to be purified and ripened. Naturally, this occurs not without some pain. But the deceased who are undergoing purification have not lost all communication with the Church of Christ. We can assist them by our prayers, Masses and sacrifices. In the Apostles' Creed, we declare, "We believe in the communion of saints." The saints in heaven, the members of the pilgrim Church and the souls in the "place" of purification together form one great community, the center of which is Jesus Christ. The binding force of this community is the Holy Spirit, and its members, hand in hand, interceding for one another and helping one another, move forward toward the happy future of the entire world.

Because the world has a future, and because this future is an eternal one, the road of the world wends into the life of God Himself. Jesus promised, "I shall come again" (Jn 14:3). He comes daily with the invisible promptings of His grace; He comes in the sacraments; He comes in the guise of our fellow men, who are waiting for our help. But there will be one more coming of Christ, and this coming will mark the end of the pilgrimage of the human race through the centuries. It will mark the end of this world, the final day of judgment (Mt 25:31–46). No one but the Father knows the day or the hour (Mt 24:36). We await this day, however, looking forward in hope toward the coming in glory of our Savior, Jesus Christ. There will then be a new heaven and a new earth (Rev 21:1), and even nature itself will then share in the glorious freedom of the children of God (Rom 8:20–21). By the grace of God, together with the Son, we shall see the Father face to face. United with the Holy Spirit, we shall love the Father and all things in Him. Thus will God become all in all. Love will become all in all.

Mary, Star of Our Hope

God has given us Mary, the mother of His only Son. He has given her to us as the wondrous mirror of our eternal hope, the most beautiful flower of the human race. Mary was the young girl chosen by God. On her He showered His grace from the first moment of her conception (the Immaculate Conception) and singled her out to be the mother of His Incarnate Son. Jesus had no earthly father. God wanted to show that, although Jesus was truly a man, His incarnation was not the work of the power of man, but a gift of God's love. It was perfectly correct for Jesus to address only God, the heavenly Father, as "My dear Father." Since "nothing is impossible with God" (Lk 1:36), the wondrous power of the Holy Spirit made Mary, the virgin, the mother of Jesus. The flower of her virginity blossomed only for God, and she became a mother, loving with the warmth of the dearest mother on earth. Two beautiful realities became one in the Virgin-Mother. Mary believed "what was spoken to her from the Lord" (Lk 1:45) and answered the angel of the Lord with the words, "Behold, I am the handmaid of the Lord; let it be done to me according to Your word" (Lk 1:38).

It was Mary who stood at the foot of the cross of her Son.

Even then and there, it was she who believed in Him (Jn 19:25–27). She was present with the apostles on the first Pentecost when the Holy Spirit filled them all with a new fire (Acts 1:14; 2:1). And when her silent, modest, unsensational, earthly life came to an end, she was taken up to paradise by her Son so that she might participate in His resurrection. These mysteries are brought together in the beautiful ancient prayer, the "Hail Mary," and are meditated upon when we recite the rosary.

Mary is the perfect example of a human being showered with the love of God, redeemed by Christ and filled with the Holy Spirit. She is the most perfect member and the prototype of the Church. Even in heaven she does not remain idle. She takes to her mother's heart not only Jesus, but all of us, the brothers and sisters of Jesus. We are all of us her children. She unceasingly prays for us "now and at the hour of our death."

The mother of our God and Savior, Jesus Christ, is our mother and heavenly patroness, the mirror of God's love, the mirror of the heart of Jesus. Her motherly heart teaches us the same truth that Jesus proclaimed in His life, death and resurrection: "God is good; His mercy endures forever" (Ps 118). To be a Christian means just that: to believe this and to live by this faith now and for all eternity.

REFLECTION AND DISCUSSION

1. How do people think about the future? With hope? With fear? With despair? Are there different kinds of hope? What is it that Christians hope for? Is Christian hope actually giving joy and purpose to my life?

2. In what way does the Christian belief that only love and its work remain forever affect my thoughts and actions? Does my life in any way resemble those servants who were eagerly await-

ing the coming of their Lord with burning lamps in their hands
(Lk 12:35–38)?

3. Speaking about the eternal future of the world, St. Paul
says, "God will be all in all" (1 Cor 15:28). What is his meaning?
What is it that I can do to help bring the world and myself closer
to this blessed end?

4. What is the relationship of Mary to God the Father, to
Jesus Christ, and to us? How does the mystery of her mother-
hood bring the mercy of God close to us? She herself foretold
that all generations would call her "blessed." Do I genuinely
think of her as really "blessed"? Am I sharing in her faith and
her obedience in such a way that I, too, will be called blessed?
Am I listening with joy to those words of wisdom spoken to me
by my mother Mary: "Let it be done unto me—let it be"?

Bibliography

Chapter 1

Congar, Y. *Jesus Christ.* New York: Herder and Herder, 1966.

Durrwell, F. X. *The Resurrection: A Biblical Study.* London: Sheed and Ward, 1964.

Dulles, A. *Apologetics and the Biblical Christ.* Westminster, Md.: Newman Press, 1966.

———. *Revelation Theology.* New York: Herder and Herder, 1969.

John Paul II. Encyclical *Dives in misericordia.*

———. Encyclical *Redemptor hominis.*

Kasper, W. *An Introduction to Christian Faith.* New York: Paulist Press, 1981.

———. *Jesus the Christ.* London: Burns and Oates, 1976.

Kelly, J.N.D. *Early Christian Doctrines.* New York: Harper and Row, 1960.

Lane, Dermot A. *The Reality of Jesus: An Essay in Christology.* New York: Paulist Press, 1975.

O'Collins, G. *Fundamental Theology.* New York: Paulist Press, 1981.

Quesnell, Q. *This Good News: An Introduction to the Christian Theology of the New Testament.* London: Geoffrey Chapman, 1964.

Rahner, K. (ed.). *Encyclopedia of Theology: A Concise Sacramentum Mundi.* London: Burns and Oates, 1975.

Ratzinger, J. *Introduction to Christianity.* New York: Herder and Herder, 1970.

Schnackenburg, R. *The Moral Teaching of the New Testament.* New York: Herder and Herder, 1965.

Schürmann, H. *Praying With Christ: The "Our Father" for Today.* New York: Herder and Herder, 1964.

Tripole, M.R. *The Jesus Event and Our Response.* New York: Alba House, 1980.

Vatican Council II. *Constitution on Divine Revelation.*

Verhalen, P.A. *Faith in a Secularized World.* New York: Paulist Press, 1976.

Chapter 2

Congar, Y. *Lay People in the Church.* Westminster, Md.: Newman Press, 1965.

———. *The Mystery of the Church.* Baltimore: Helicon Press, 1965.

de Lubac, H. *Catholicism. A Study of Dogma in Relation to the Corporative Destiny of Mankind.* London: Burns and Oates, 1950.

———. *The Splendor of the Church.* New York: Sheed and Ward, 1955.

Dulles, A. *Models of the Church.* New York: Doubleday, 1974.

Kloppenburg, B. *The Ecclesiology of Vatican II.* Chicago: Franciscan Herald Press, 1974.

McKenzie, J.L. *Authority in the Church.* New York: Sheed and Ward, 1966.

Monden, L. *Faith: Can Man Still Believe?* New York: Sheed and Ward, 1970.

Rahner, K. *Foundations of Christian Faith. An Introduction to the Idea of Christianity.* New York: Seabury Press, 1978.

Schineller, Peter *et al. Why the Church?* New York: Paulist Press, 1977.

Schmaus, M. *Dogma.* (six volumes) London: Sheed and Ward, 1968–77.

Schnackenburg, R. *The Church in the New Testament.* New York: Herder and Herder, 1966.

———. *The Moral Teaching of the New Testament.* New York: Herder and Herder, 1971.

Vatican Council II. *Constitution on the Church.*

————. Pastoral Constitution on the Church in the Modern World.

————. Decree on Ecumenism.

Vorgrimler, Herbert *et al. Commentary on the Documents of Vatican II.* (five volumes) New York: Herder and Herder, 1967–69.

Chapter 3

Bausch, William J. *A New Look at the Sacraments.* Notre Dame: Fides Press, 1977.

Boros, L. *Christian Prayer.* New York: Seabury Press, 1976.

Bouyer, L. *Liturgy and Piety.* Notre Dame: University of Notre Dame Press, 1955.

Brown, R. *Priest and Bishop: Biblical Reflections.* New York: Paulist Press, 1970.

Ganoczy, A. *Becoming Christian.* New York: Paulist Press, 1976.

Hellwig, M. *The Meaning of the Sacraments.* Dayton: Pfaum, 1972.

John Paul II. Encyclical *Laborem exercens.*

Kavanagh. A. *The Shape of Baptism: The Rite of Christian Initiation.* New York: Pueblo Publishing, 1978.

Kilmartin, E.J. *The Eucharist in the Primitive Church.* Englewood Cliffs: Prentice-Hall, 1965.

Powers, J.M. *Eucharistic Theology.* New York: Seabury Press, 1967.

Rahner, K. *Everyday Faith.* New York: Herder and Herder, 1968.

————. *Meditations on the Sacraments.* New York: Seabury Press, 1977.

————. *The Church and the Sacraments.* New York: Herder and Herder, 1963.

Schillebeeckx, E. *Christ, the Sacrament of the Encounter with God.* New York: Sheed and Ward, 1963.

Sullivan, C.S. (ed). *Readings in Sacramental Theology.* Englewood Cliffs: Prentice-Hall, 1964.

Tartre, R.A. *The Eucharist Today.* New York: P.J. Kenedy and Sons, 1967.

Taylor, M.J. *The Sacraments*. New York: Alba House, 1981.

Vagaggini, C. *Theological Dimension of the Liturgy*. Collegeville: Liturgical Press, 1976.

Vaillancourt, R. *Towards a Renewal of Sacramental Theology*. Collegeville: Liturgical Press, 1979.

Worgul, G.S. *From Magic to Metaphor*. New York: Paulist Press, 1980.

Chapter 4

Fortmann, E.J. *Everlasting Life After Death*. New York: Alba House, 1976.

Gleason, R. *The World to Come*. New York: Sheed and Ward, 1958.

Ratzinger, J. and J. Auer. *Eschatologie, Tod und Ewiges Leben*. Regensburg, 1977.

Schnackenburg, R. *God's Rule and Kingdom*. London: Nelson, 1963.

Simpson, M. *The Theology of Death and Eternal Life*. Notre Dame: Fides Press, 1971.